WCSK

WHAT CHRISTIANS SHOULD KNOW

THE SIMPLE AND EASY BIBLE STUDY GUIDE TO BASIC CHRISTIAN BELIEFS AND BASIC CHRISTIAN DOCTRINE

Dr. C. H. E. Sadaphal

Copyright © 2015 C. H. E. Sadaphal

Scriptures taken from the Holy Bible, New International Version®, NIV®. Copyright © 1973, 1978, 1984, 2011 by Biblica, Inc.™ Used by permission of Zondervan. All rights reserved worldwide. www.zondervan.com. The "NIV" and "New International Version" are trademarks registered in the United States Patent and Trademark Office by Biblica, Inc.™

Scripture quotations taken from the New American Standard Bible® (NASB),

Copyright © 1960, 1962, 1963, 1968, 1971, 1972, 1973,1975, 1977, 1995 by The Lockman Foundation. Used by permission. www.Lockman.org

To Nigel Elisha:

I strive to be good so that you can be great.

Table of Contents

PREFACE i
THE FIVE CORE DOCTRINES OF THE CHRISTIAN FAITH: vii
CHAPTER I: INTRODUCTION & WHAT CHRISTIANITY IS 1
CHAPTER II: WHO GOD IS 11
CHAPTER III: THE BIBLE 29
CHAPTER IV: CREATION & SIN 61
CHAPTER V: THE INCARNATION, LIFE, DEATH, AND
RESURRECTION OF JESUS CHRIST 87
CHAPTER VI: COVENANT 113
CHAPTER VII: GRACE AND STEWARDSHIP 131
CHAPTER VIII: THE CHURCH 149
CHAPTER IX: REGENERATION 167
CHAPTER X: WORSHIP 181

Preface

In the book of I Kings, we are introduced to the prophet Elijah for the first time. This legendary figure arrives on the scene at a bleak time in Israel's history. Drought and famine have struck the land, forcing even the wealthy to scavenge for food, much like dogs. The king and queen blatantly defy God's commandments and openly sanction the worship of false deities. Those deities include the alleged gods of rain and agriculture during a time of no rain and starvation. God is trying to tell the people something, but they choose not to listen. As a result, God calls Elijah to serve as His human instrument to turn the people away from apostasy and back toward Him.

It is for this reason that we find Elijah atop Mt. Carmel in I Kings, chapter 18. The people of Israel are gathered there to see a showdown among the gods. On one side stands Elijah—he alone stands for the one true God. On the other side are 850 prophets of false gods. At stake is the heart of the nation of Israel. The wager centers on who can call out and receive an answer from heaven. If the false prophets receive an answer, then their gods win. If Elijah does so, then god really is God—Jehovah or Yahweh; the God of the Bible; the God of Israel; the God of Abraham, Isaac, and Jacob.

On top of the mountain, in the midst of the confrontation, Elijah then asks one of the most powerful questions in the entire Bible to all those looking on: "How long will you waver between two opinions?" (I Kings 18:21a, NIV).

Although Elijah was outnumbered; although he was mocked and ridiculed; although he lived on the fringes of society; and although he was regarded as "out of touch," "antiquated," and "backward," he stood for truth and had a single-minded dedication to the LORD. Elijah couldn't help himself because his name literally means, "My God is Yahweh." He acted based on his God-given identity, so no matter how "unpopular" the truth was, he stood firm *in* the truth. Elijah fully understood that when you live in a world that doesn't honor God, you will be misunderstood and labeled in derogatory ways. Turning toward God and resistance actually go hand in hand, and although the messenger is human, *the message* is omnipotent.

Elijah represents all those in modern times unafraid to stand for the truth in a world full of opinions. Just as the prophet did, we find ourselves fighting an uphill battle in which many so-called religious leaders have adopted a more "digestible" version of the gospel to attract followers and secure secondary gain. Moreover, just as King Ahab and Queen Jezebel did in the time of Elijah, many in positions of power and authority now openly sanction syncretism and half-truths to formalize their power and solidify loyalty. These clever individuals need not preach heresy—they simply substitute for the whole truth a vacuous, Christ-less form of subjective "spirituality" in which faith has become what *I* want to believe. What is said from the pulpit therefore is indistinguishable from what is said in a corporate boardroom, at a self-help seminar, or at the paid conference of a motivational speaker. Subsequently, in contemporary America, *spirituality* is on the rise, while *Christianity* is in steep decline.* This situation comes as no surprise; at our core, we are not physical beings trying to adapt to our spiritual selves. We are image bearers of God, spiritual beings attempting to adjust to the physical world. Ecclesiastes 3:11 says that God has placed eternity in our hearts, so it is no wonder that humanity endlessly searches for something bigger, deeper, and more meaningful.

---

* In fact, the Pew Research Center reports that the share of adults in the United States who label themselves Christian has declined since 2007 from 78.4% to 70.6%. This represents a decline of about 5 million adults and affects nearly all major Christian traditions and denominations. At the same time, the amount of those "unaffiliated" with any religion has *increased* nearly 7% since 2007 to number a total of 56 million people. This figure represents roughly 23% of adults. In other words, in 2015 in America, roughly 1 out of every 4 adults is either an atheist, agnostic, or "nothing in particular."

American spirituality is built upon the foundation of *me*, but a house of faith built upon the foundation of self will not stand. In this house, God must compete for my attention and provide personalized incentives. If His performance falls short, I simply move on to the next idol. Rules become nothing more than burdensome inconveniences and a threat to my rugged individualism.

Accordingly, before Elijah goes down in history as a great prophet who turns the people's hearts back to God, those in power label him a "troubler," an instigator, and a bothersome menace. Similarly, in the twenty-first century, if you're not willing to be "controversial," then you're not willing to stand for God and His Word. The Bible shows clearly that obedience to the LORD has always been a countercultural choice in direct opposition to the status quo. Moses fought against the obsession with inhumane and endless production in the Egyptian economic system, Micah warned that exploitation of others in climbing the ladder of success would bring judgment and ruin, and Jesus informed the religious "authorities" of His time that the accepted interpretation of the Scriptures was a perversion of the truth. Subsequently, in 2015, Christians squabble over many extraneous things, failing to realize that sound doctrine is *the* fight always worth fighting.

Herein lies the problem with subjective religion and multiple opinions: when you spend so much time hopping from branch to branch, you begin to lose focus on *your* real opinion. Accordingly, you become numb both to sin *and* to God. This numbness leads to apathy and the inability to take a firm stand on anything, which is exactly why evil can casually say, "Whatever..." to the question, "How long will you waver?" The response in the text says, "But the people said nothing" (I Kings 18:21b, NIV).

Furthermore, Elijah didn't ask his famous question to atheists. He didn't ask agnostics. He didn't ask any group you might consider "sinners." He asked *Israelites*. He asked a people who knew God, who were aware of God's law, who had a national identity exclusively because of God, and who were living in a land promised to them by God. The story of Elijah isn't an indictment of all those "heathens" who do not know Jesus. It *is* an indictment of those who label themselves Christians or who are members of Christ's church. Throughout the Bible, God always judges those who know Him first, *and then* He deals with those on the "outside." Before we accuse others of anything, we ought to look at the person in the mirror first and foremost. Otherwise, we have promoted ourselves to the position of deity.

A person who refuses to waver between opinions has an unchangeable Christian identity firmly rooted in Jesus Christ. This Christian refuses to compromise, is unafraid of the trouble and challenges that come with transformation, and boldly proclaims that Jehovah is God in a world that is apathetic to sin, responsibility, and accountability. This identity is a fixed point of reference in a world full of confusion; it is the persistent, pervasive, all-encompassing force that steers a person's mind, thoughts, words, and actions. Identity always *precedes* behavior; all action stems and *proceeds from* this core sense of self, and that self is formed in the image of God.

For those who have been wondering what happened with Elijah, well, God allowed him to win the showdown. The LORD sent down fire from heaven and revealed the true God, bringing everyone to their knees in recognition of the Almighty. As for the false prophets, they were all destroyed.

At the end of the day, neither God nor the Bible needs to be defended by any human being, but susceptible humans need protection against the malicious vipers that purposely pervert, exploit, distort, and capitalize on the Word of God. Jesus never intended for spiritual tyranny to burden the souls of His sheep, nor did He ever intend for His "shepherds" to enslave all those He set free on the cross.

What Christians Should Know (WCSK) is meant to guide you into and along the path of Christ and humbly attempts to mimic what He did for people: to liberate them. It is designed to empower *you* to read, study, understand, and become familiar with the incarnate Word of God for yourself. By knowing and understanding the truth, you will never succumb to false doctrine or the notion that "sort-of-the-truth" is *the* truth. As it says in the beginning of the *Didache*, "There are two Ways, one of Life and one of Death, and there is a great difference between the two Ways." Anything other than Jesus Christ leads to death. *He* is the path of Life.

WCSK aims to begin the process of transforming *believers in* Christ into *disciples of* Christ as they walk that path. Jesus says, "Go therefore and make *disciples* [emphasis added] of all the nations, baptizing them in the name of the Father and the Son and the Holy Spirit, teaching them to observe all that I commanded you; and lo, I am with you always, even to the end of the age" (Matthew 28:19-20, NASB). *Matheteuo*, the Greek word for *disciple*, is very interesting because it simultaneously implies an inner role as a pupil and an outward role as a teacher. By implication, to teach well, *you* must first have an ironclad grasp on the subject matter.

What if people came up to you in the street and asked, "What do you believe, and why do you believe it?" Could you answer the questions? What if they wanted you to explain to them the basic, core doctrines of the Christian faith? Could you do so? Could you direct them on where to go? What if someone said, "The Bible is too complicated. I need something to guide me"? What if someone wanted to take a step toward Christ but felt unworthy, intimidated, or overwhelmed by "doing church"? What if you desire to do all the "right" things but often feel like the things you hear don't relate to you or you can't understand how what's preached on Sunday actually matters in your life? What if you go through the religious motions because your parents tell you to but have never taken an honest look at it all *for yourself*?

WCSK is a vehicle for individual and institutional change. It is the nutrition for starving Christians who suffer from doctrinal apathy and the proper sustenance of enduring Biblical truth for believers. It is intended to be accessible, practical, and applicable to everyone. *WCSK* challenges Christians to rethink *what they think they know* and invites all curious minds to discover (or rediscover) the Word of God, challenging our fascination with cultural fads and moralism. The work forces us to reorient our spiritual walk and aims to expand and enlarge the pool of faithful, eager, and willing followers of Christ who have become so empowered, invigorated, and set ablaze that they can't help but spread the good news to others.

Of all my father's sermons, my favorite posed one simple question: "Is your salvation secure?" On the Day of Judgment, the only person to be held accountable before God for all your wrongdoing is *you*. There will be no excuses, no scapegoats, and no loopholes. It is for this reason that we must never, ever take our walk of faith lightly but rather with the full recognition of the depravity of sin and the irrevocable consequences of leading a life without Jesus at the center. As the apostle Paul wrote, "Work out your salvation with fear and trembling; for it is God who is at work in you, both to will and to work for His good pleasure" (Philippians 2:12-13, NASB).

I sincerely hope you enjoy and are enriched by the lessons.

May God richly bless you and guide you in your studies.

"Your word is a lamp to my feet and a light to my path" (Psalm 119:105).

Dr. Charles Haddon Elijah Sadaphal
April 2015

Appendix

The Five Core Doctrines of the Christian Faith:

1. There is one God, yet God is three distinct Persons, each of whom is fully God: Father, Son (Jesus), and Holy Spirit.
2. Jesus Christ is fully God and fully man in one person.
3. Jesus bore the penalty of sin in His death, He was a substitute sacrifice for us all, and that substitution atoned for humanity, thereby reconciling us back to God.
4. Jesus was crucified and died on the cross, and on the third day, He rose from the dead.
5. We are saved by grace alone and through faith in Jesus Christ alone.

CHAPTER I
INTRODUCTION &
WHAT CHRISTIANITY IS

What does this series aim to achieve?

It aims to give those who label themselves "Christians" a basic understanding of what they should know and what Christianity is, based solely on the fundamental concepts that the Bible teaches us. This series aims to educate, empower and vitalize the willing disciples of Christ so that they can enhance their own understanding *and then* minister to others by spreading the good news. The theme of this series is "faith seeking understanding." The theme verse is Titus 2:1: "But as for you, speak the things which are fitting for sound doctrine."

All scriptures are taken from The New American Standard Bible (NASB) unless otherwise noted. Further, Biblical references are examples and are in no way exhaustive. The series *What Christians Should Know* (WCSK) also is not a complete reference but is meant to provide basic beliefs, principles, and doctrines of the Christian faith. All of the lessons are best used as a general guide as you engage in your own Bible study.

I. The Crisis

In the 2008 American Religious Identification Survey (ARIS), 76% of Americans self-identified as Christian and 34% identified as "Born Again or Evangelical." 15% of those polled identified as atheist, agnostic or having no religious preference. Significantly, ARIS determined that the challenge to American Christianity "does not come from other religions but rather a rejection of all forms of organized religion."

In the same year, the Pew Research Center conducted a poll that found that, among American Christians, 52% believed that "at least some non-Christian faiths can lead to eternal life." Furthermore, of those in this majority, 80% could "name at least one non-Christian faith that can do so." Only 29% of those polled believed that "my religion is the one, true faith leading to eternal life." Six percent of the respondents did not know who would achieve eternal life or refused to answer.

In 2014, the Barna Group and the American Bible Society completed a report called "The State of the Bible." According to this report, four out of five adults (81%) said that morality was on the decline and nearly one-third (29%) cited the lack of Bible reading as the primary cause. The study also revealed that, among American adults:

(i) 81% considered themselves "highly, moderately, or somewhat" knowledgeable about the Bible, yet 43% of this group was unable to name the Bible's first five books. (This number rose to 69% among Protestants.)

(ii) 88% said their household owned a Bible, but nearly half of adults (46%) read the Bible *no more frequently* than two to three times a year.

(iii) A significant number of people believed that the Bible *was silent* on the following issues: pornography (34%), gambling (23%), same-sex relationships (21%) and the repression of women (24%).

(iv) Half (50%) "agreed strongly or agreed somewhat" that the Bible, the Quran and the Book of Mormon were all different expressions of the *same* spiritual truths.

All of this information points to one disturbing conclusion: Biblical illiteracy is rampant and people don't know what they think they know, nor do they understand what they believe. This is a crisis of insurmountable proportions, considering what's at stake. To this I add my own perception that one of the greatest threats to modern Christianity and those *within* the church is religious pluralism (resulting from Biblical illiteracy) and the greatest threat to those *without* is syncretism. Both of these subtle, seemingly innocuous and voluntary forces have managed to do more damage than any army, evil despot or oppressive power in the contemporary era.

II. What Does This All Mean in Practical Terms?

People may say that they believe in God, but that does not necessarily mean that they have an understanding of who God is and what God says. For this reason, this series has three goals in mind:

(1) To bring clarity to those who do not know Christ using an unbiased, free and widely available means. In this way, the series will share with them the basic facts about Christ, the Bible and Christian doctrine. No matter who they are, where they are or what they already believe, they will have unrestricted access to this knowledge at any time.

(2) To combat Biblical illiteracy among those who are somewhat familiar with the Bible, but have not taken the time to sit down with the Word, study it, reflect upon it and become dedicated students of it. The term "Christian" can mean many different things in modern society and this series will challenge believers to scrutinize what they already know and what they think they already know about the Bible. Faith should be grounded in timeless Biblical truth and all believers must consequently have a clear and comprehensive understanding of *what* they believe and *why* they believe it. This is an issue that transcends the emotions and requires earnest, deep and honest introspection.

(3) To nurture *fides quaerens intellectum* or "faith seeking understanding." Some people think they can figure God out on their own without consulting *the* authoritative source. Thus, for them, the ultimate truth is not based on external authority but on internal intuition. Emotion is a part of the human experience, but we must engage reason and intellect *in pursuit* of God in order to deepen and expand our understanding of the One Whom we serve.

Belief always comes first and ultimate wisdom is always revealed, never acquired. While the Christian walk is much more than a mental exercise, it certainly is a mental challenge. The fact remains that details need to be learned, principles mastered, truths discerned and stories told correctly. This is why, in the *Proslogion*, Anselm said, "I do not try, Lord, to attain Your lofty heights, because my understanding is in no way equal to it. But I do desire to understand Your truth a little, that truth that my heart believes and loves. For I do not seek to understand so that I may believe; but I believe so that I may understand."[1]

I hope to reveal that God is a God who transcends race, gender, nation, creed or any other category: A God of one tribe, one race, one culture, one ethnicity, one people or one geographic area is not in fact God, but a construct developed to serve ideological ends.

Now, are there problems in the modern church and with Christians? Of course. The church is an institution that can help people *and* that can harm them. The world often uses the followers of Christ as a barometer for religion's validity, but they should look at Christians through a different lens. It is *because* we are all imperfect and in need of help that we need the grace and strength of Christ in order to work through our human failings. When I walk into an emergency room, I expect to see the sick and when I walk into a gym, I expect to see the out-of-shape. This doesn't reflect the deficiencies of the institutions, but the fallibility of human nature.

---

[1] "Proslogion," St. Anselm Institute, last modified May 6, 2015, accessed June 24, 2015, http://www.stanselminstitute.org/files/AnselmProslogion.pdf

One must understand that God works through messy and complicated human experience in order to produce a flesh-and-bones intimacy with our reality. This intimacy doesn't shy away from tough problems, but works through them. It is for this reason that the Bible depicts love, mercy, grace, family, triumph, peace and liberation, as well as murder, genocide, rape, lust, incest, oppression, social and economic injustice and war. Hence, the Bible is powerful and enriching *because* it's about real life and tells us about real people with real problems and issues. Love is very messy and the Bible is a love story about a caring Father who incessantly chases after His fallen creation in order to bring them back to Him.

Reading the Bible daily and engaging in an intimate relationship with God is one of the only ways to develop *your* own faith and understanding. One of the greatest dangers in the modern world entails allowing someone else to give you his or her theology and passively accepting it as true. This is not to trivialize tradition or to dismiss orthodoxy. In fact, any bold leap forward in the Christian walk is not a revolutionary shift away from the Bible, but an earnest look *back at* the Scriptures—in order to move forward, we must first go back. The issue, then, isn't *whether* we ought to honor tradition. Rather, we should determine *which* tradition will give us life and is therefore worth our total being and complete submission. That tradition is the Bible, the Word of God.

This is a critical step for each person to take because every person who seeks to know the Word must become a disciple of the Word. Education drives knowledge and this praxis requires discipline, focus, determination and strength. Fragile, unintelligible and unexamined beliefs will lead to weak disciples, weak dedication, weak religion and a weak church.

Doctrine means a belief or a set of beliefs that an institution teaches, whereas theology entails the study of beliefs and the study of the nature of God. The root source of all Christian doctrine is the Bible. However, some groups may not accept the Bible as a whole, may emphasize one part or may de-emphasize another. Different denominations will therefore tend to have different traditions and there is nothing inherently wrong with any of that. However, Jesus did not intend for the church to inflict spiritual tyranny on believers while burdening them with the yoke of the institution, nor did He intend for a superstructure of man-made elements to keep people away from Him. Accordingly, the approach I will be taking is that the Word of God is divinely inspired and written by humans through the power and revelation of the Holy Spirit. I do not intend for the doctrine that I teach to serve any ideological end. Rather, I want it to be as true to the *Biblical* tradition as possible and to take each subject and accept it as truth, cognizant that this truth comes in the context of the Bible as a whole. The whole must form the basis for the interpretation of the part and not vice versa.

III. What Is Christianity?

The simplest answer boils down to two words: Jesus Christ.

What Christians should know is that Christianity *is* Christ, Who *is* the centerpiece of the entire Christian faith. Salvation is possible because of Christ. He is the ultimate expression of God's love for humanity and He represents God's atonement of all of our sins so that we (humankind) can reconcile with God and restore a proper relationship with Him.

Christians should know that God created us out of His abundance and *not* out of a lack or need. He defined His ownership and dominion over everything by giving it all away.

What Christians should know is that Christianity is the final and ultimate narrative of *how* and *why* we all began. Our beginning was not some impersonal, random event that resulted from nothing, but the direct result of God's divine and conscious decision to bring light, life and order into our universe.

Christians should know that Christianity gives the most comprehensive explanation of who we truly are. It is the source of our legitimate identities as sons and daughters of God, formed in His image. It also satisfies, through Christ, the eternal yearning that we have to worship and to fulfill the deepest, most sincere, most fundamental desires of our being.

Christians should know that Christianity reveals to us that the world we live in is not the final testament of our existence. Because of sin, it is a temporary and highly imperfect representation of what was previously flawless. Christianity points directly toward Christ and His example for us of how to live in accordance with God's commands.

What Christians should know is that one of the mainstays of the Christian faith is the Bible. The Bible is more than a book and is God's divine word, revealed to humans through verbal plenary inspiration. The Bible is what God wanted us to know, learn and understand about Him, not as a means to deter or hinder us, but so that we would live our lives abundantly. We are the creation and He is The Creator; he did not give us these rules and regulations in malice. Rather, he sought to protect us, just as a loving father instructs his son and guides him away from harm.

What Christians should know is that God is just and merciful and that there is a constant tension between these two qualities. Because God is perfectly just, He can't simply say "Never mind" to sin. That would contradict His nature and diminish His character. Despite our actions, mercy triumphs over judgment. God's love compelled Him to incarnate as a Man (Jesus) for our sake—that is, in order to reconcile with humanity by re-creating creation and turning the corruptible (humans) back into the incorruptible, God required nothing less than His own substance. By willingly sacrificing Himself, He saved all of us.

Christians should know that John 3:16 says, "For God so loved the world, that He gave His only begotten son, that whoever believes in Him shall not perish, but have eternal life."

Christians should know that Luke 19:10 says that Christ came into this world "to seek and to save that which was lost." This has two implications. First, *seeking* is an active, engrossing practice that looks towards others instead of working against them. Secondly, those involved in *saving* must, at the very least, have a basic understanding of the subject matter on which they're ministering.

Christians should know that Psalm 119:105 says, "Your word is a lamp to my feet and a light to my path." Without the light of Christ and without the Bible, we are doomed to dwell in darkness, confused and alone with no one to guide us. It is *only and irrefutably* through Jesus Christ that anyone can walk in the light, back toward God.

Christians should know that, in John 14:6, Jesus says, "I am the way, the truth, and the life; no one comes to the Father but through Me."

What Christians should know is that the concept of the Trinitarian God of the Bible is a unique truth claim. This distinguishes Christianity from other ideologies, religions and forms of spirituality.

What Christians should know is that on multiple occasions, Jesus Christ said, "I am God."[2] Period. There is no grey area, no question and no doubt. No other (legitimate and sane) leader of a major religion has ever claimed to be God. This bold truth was so powerful that Jesus willingly died for it. To avoid death, all He would have had to do was recant his statement, but He never did. He died for the truth.

Christians should know that God loves humanity very much. Thankfully for us, however much we curse Him and reject Him, God plays by His rules and not human ones. So no matter who you are or what you've done, your Heavenly Father will never turn His back on you. You are His child, formed in His image and destined to conquer darkness with the light and to boldly proclaim your new Christ-centered identity. This in no way diminishes the destructive power of sin, nor does it dismiss obedience. As Dietrich Bonhoeffer has said, grace is not "cheap." It is costly—involving Christ, repentance, the cross, discipleship and suffering. This is why, in *The Cost of Discipleship*, Bonhoeffer says, "With an abstract idea it is possible to enter into a relation of formal knowledge, to become enthusiastic about it, and

---

[2] Mark 14:61-64; John 10:30-33, 36-39

perhaps even put it into practice; but it can never be followed in personal obedience. Christianity without the living Christ is inevitably Christianity without discipleship, and Christianity without discipleship is always Christianity without Christ."[3]

IV. The Importance of Understanding What You Know, What You Believe and Why You Believe It.

In the modern world, "truth" no longer has any objective value and depends on what "feels" right or seems to move us the best. There is certainty in Christ; that is a real-life, tangible incarnation of truth. It is so real and genuine that you can touch, feel and get splintered by the cross on which He was crucified. This isn't a truth for me alone; it is meant for you too. Indeed, it is *the* Truth that does not change under pressure. It invites you to take a look for yourself and embrace the life-giving power that is the Bible.

For as long as I can remember, I've known *about* Christ and *about* the church. However, it was only when I immersed myself in the Word that I truly began to hear. As a consequence, from hearing came faith and from faith came understanding.

I love and follow Christ because He met me in a time of strife and used the crisis to show me that all the knowledge I had amassed, all the wisdom I thought I had and all the "security" I had acquired were formless and void. They were unable to yield any dividends beyond the present, provide comfort beyond the temporal and satisfy my internal yearning for something that transcended my reality. Make no mistake, I didn't experience a miraculous "shining light" followed by a perfect existence. Rather, my Christian walk is a slow, persistent, day-by-day process and I experience incremental changes in my pursuit to be more like Him. It is a continual process of regeneration that transforms me from the person I am into the person I know I can be, empowered solely by the Holy Spirit, through Christ, to the Father.

---

[3] Dietrich Bonhoeffer, *The Cost of Discipleship* (New York: Touchstone, 1959), 59.

CHAPTER II
WHO GOD IS

What Christians should know is that in order to live an obedient life and enter into a relationship with God, one must have a comprehensive understanding of who God is.

In contemplating God, a logical first question to ask is, "Does God Exist?" Once that uncertainty is successfully addressed, the next question to ponder is, "Who is God?" The focus of this lesson will be on the second question, assuming that all of us have already taken the path in favor of theism, have been illuminated in support of the truth, and now would like to learn more about Whom we serve. In order to address the first question, I will direct you to "For Further Study" at the end of this chapter.

The first place to start when talking about what Christians should know is God. After all, that's where the Bible starts. Genesis 1:1 says, "In the beginning, God ..."

Thus, all Christians should be able to answer the question, "Who is my God?"

As with any other relationship, the closer two people become, the more each gets to know about the other. It is important to realize, however, that God can be known, but this feat is not accomplished strictly by human means, but is part of the revelation of God *to us*. So, a person sitting alone in a room in deep thought won't be able to "know" God—He *cannot* be known through human wisdom alone.[4] The first requirement is an earnest desire to know, and then comes engagement with the Scriptures, where true knowledge of God is to be found. Any attempt, then, to understand God without referencing the

---

[4] I Corinthians 1:21

Scriptures will lead to suppression of the truth, futile thinking, and darkened hearts.[5]

Hence, in Matthew 11:27 Jesus says, "All things have been handed over to Me by My Father, and no one knows the Son except the Father; nor does anyone know the Father except the Son, and anyone to whom *the Son wills to reveal Him.*" Romans 1:19 says, "Because that which is known about God is evident within them, for God made it evident *to* them." (In both verses the italics are mine.)

With this idea also comes the recognition that we, as temporal human beings, cannot ever *fully* grasp God, because He is greater than us and eternal. This makes sense because we are the creation, so of course there will be concepts and attributes about Him that are beyond comprehension. This is why in Isaiah 55:9, God speaks through the prophet and says, "For as the heavens are higher than the earth, so are My ways higher than your ways, and My thoughts than your thoughts." The Psalmist says that God's "greatness is unsearchable,"[6] His "understanding is infinite,"[7] and the LORD'S "knowledge is too wonderful for me; It is too high, I cannot attain it."[8] In I Corinthians 2:11-12, the apostle Paul says, "Even so the thoughts of God no one knows except the Spirit of God. Now we have received, not the spirit of the world, but the Spirit who is from God, so that we may know the things freely given to us by God."

There is a tremendous wealth of information about who God is in the Bible. The Bible teaches us that God is love,[9] light,[10] Spirit, [11] just, [12] omnipresent, [13] omnipotent, [14] omniscient, [15]

---

[5] Romans 1:18-21
[6] Psalm 145:3
[7] Psalm 147:5
[8] Psalm 139:6
[9] I John 4:8; John 3:16, 17:24
[10] I John 1:5
[11] John 4:24
[12] Romans 3:26
[13] Jeremiah 23:24; Psalm 139:7-10
[14] Matthew 19:26; Luke 1:37; Psalm 24:8, 115:3
[15] I John 3:20; Jeremiah 1:5

eternal,[16] wise,[17] timeless,[18] merciful,[19] holy,[20] blameless,[21] self-existent[22] (meaning God is un-causable, or in reference to His *aseity*), righteous,[23] infinite,[24] personal (Jesus Christ), invisible[25] (but God did assume visible form, or theophany, as in Genesis 18), knowledgeable,[26] truthful,[27] faithful,[28] good,[29] peaceful,[30] slow to anger and patient,[31] the Creator,[32] graceful,[33] jealous,[34] wrathful,[35] willful,[36] blessed,[37] beautiful,[38] sovereign,[39] and unchangeable.[40] God's whole being is inclusive of all these attributes, and He is simultaneously and equally all of these things.

In particular, God's omnipresence, omnipotence, and omniscience all reveal that He exists in a different way than we exist, and that very existence surpasses what we can deduce from the rules of the natural world. He is qualitatively different from us.

The word "unchangeable" means that God's character, promises, being, and purposes were, are, *and always will be* the same. This is the reason why and how we can trust in Him always—He will be good, truthful, perfect, and just eternally. He may, however, change *His response* dependent on particular

---

[16] Psalm 90:2
[17] Romans 16:27
[18] Revelation 1:8
[19] Psalm 145:9
[20] Leviticus 19:2; Isaiah 6:3
[21] Psalm 18:30
[22] John 1:3; Revelation 4:11; I Corinthians 8:6
[23] Psalm 145:17
[24] Revelation 4:8
[25] Exodus 33:20; John 1:18, 6:46; I Tim 1:17; I John 4:12
[26] Job 37:16
[27] John 17:3
[28] I Peter 4:19; II Samuel 7:28
[29] Acts 14:17; Romans 12:2; James 1:17; Psalm 107:1
[30] II Thessalonians 3:16; Philippians 4:6; I Corinthians 14:33; Galatians 5:22
[31] Romans 2:4; Nahum 1:3; Jonah 4:2; Numbers 14:18; Colossians 3:12
[32] Genesis 1:1; I John 2:15-17
[33] Romans 3:23-24; I Corinthians 15:10
[34] Exodus 34:14
[35] Exodus 32:9-10; Romans 1:18
[36] Jeremiah 29:11; I Thessalonians 5:16-18; Psalm 40:8; Ephesians 1:11; I Peter 3:17
[37] I Timothy 1:11, 6:15
[38] Psalm 27:4
[39] II Samuel 7:28; I Chronicles 29:10-13; Genesis 50:20
[40] Psalm 102:25-27; Malachi 3:6; James 1:17

circumstances. For example, in the beginning of the Book of Jonah, God intended to destroy the evil city of Nineveh because of the extreme wickedness of its people, and He sent Jonah to tell the people that judgment was coming. In response to Jonah's prophecy, in chapter 3, the text says the people of Nineveh believed God, fasted, and turned from their evil ways. In response, Jonah 3:10 says that God *relented* (in Hebrew *nacham*, meaning to be moved to pity, to have compassion, or to suffer grief) and subsequently did not harm the city or the people. So, God did not change in being both just and merciful, but He did change what He intended to do based on the situation and also consistent with His unchanging character. Other examples of God changing His mind include the successful intervention of Moses on behalf Israel's apostasy (Exodus 32:7-14) and adding 15 years to the life of Hezekiah (Isaiah 38:1-6).

Many of God's attributes are not shared (e.g., omnipresence), but others are shared with humankind in a limited way simply because we are finite creations whereas He is infinite. These shared characteristics include truthfulness, love, holiness, being just, and being merciful. So while at best, I may be somewhat merciful some of the time, God is perfectly merciful all of the time.

What Christians should know is that one of the exclusive truth claims of Christianity is that God is *both* an unlimited deity *and* a personal deity.[41] Meaning, not only is He "that-than-which-a-greater-cannot-be-thought," but He is also intimate with reality, most perfectly embodied in the Incarnation of God as Man in Jesus Christ (more on that in Chapter 5). Other religions may construct a god who is unlimited but not personal, and others may construct one who is personal but not boundless.

God also is independent of humanity and doesn't need us for anything.[42] Yet, in view of all of God's marvelous attributes, people are often confused because there are some things God cannot do. For example, God cannot lie,[43] He can't go back on his

---

[41] Isaiah 45:21
[42] Acts 17:24-25; Job 41:11
[43] Hebrews 6:18; Titus 1:2

covenantal promises,[44] He can't deny Himself,[45] He can't be tempted, nor does He tempt anyone.[46]

When I say that God doesn't need us, it's not meant to depress anyone. What that does mean, then, is that because He lacks nothing, the creation of our world and humankind came out of God's abundance. He didn't make us to fill a void, and after we have all passed away, *God will still be.* And He had meaning and purpose in creating us, so our existence was not a roll of the dice or a mishap one day in a heavenly lab. God delights in His creation,[47] created us for His glory,[48] and did so in a totally free and voluntary act, which had been predestined according to His purposes.[49]

God is a Spirit, and is therefore *sexless* and without human form. Hence, when I repeatedly refer to God as "He," that doesn't mean God is male (although Christ was a man); rather, it is a human word and concept used to denote a relationship. In fact, a myriad of anthropomorphic[50] terms are used throughout the Bible to describe God so as to use our own language to illustrate a point. God is referred to as a shepherd (Psalm 23:1), father (32:6), and physician (Exodus 15:26), while also seeing (Genesis 1:10), walking (Leviticus 26:12), remembering (Genesis 8:1), and wiping away tears (Isaiah 25:8). Examples of different emotional states include grief (Psalm 78:40), love (John 3:16), wrath (Psalm 2:5), and pity (Psalm 103:13). The Bible also refers to God's face (Exodus 33:20) and His finger (Exodus 8:19) and ears (Psalm 55:1). In a similar light, God is compared to a tower (Proverbs 18:10), a lion (Isaiah 31:4), a rock (Deuteronomy 32:4), and the sun (Psalm 84:11). With all of these things in mind, the way in which God chose to reveal Himself in relation to us is by the name Father. This is why when asked about how to

---

[44] Psalm 89:34
[45] II Timothy 2:13
[46] James 1:13
[47] Isaiah 62:4-5
[48] Isaiah 43:7
[49] Ephesians 1:11-12
[50] In other words, describing God in human terms.

pray, Jesus says in Matthew 6:9-13 to address God as "Our Father who is in Heaven."

This does not mean that God is a person in the same way that I have four limbs, get up, drink tea, and then drive to work. Rather it means that God is personal and is therefore not a remote, impersonal power.

Essential Doctrine #1: What Christians should know is that the principle of the Holy Trinity is one of the most important doctrines of the Christian faith, and it is one of the exclusive truth claims of Christianity.

What Christians should know is that there is one God, yet God is three distinct Persons, each of whom is fully God: Father, Son (Jesus), and Holy Spirit.

Also, because each member of the Trinity is fully and equally God, then one is no better than the other. Keep in mind that the word "Trinity" is never, ever, mentioned in the Bible. The word was applied by humanity in order to describe a principle pervasive in the Scriptures that is located in *both* the Old Testament and the New Testament.

A more academic and formal definition is that God is an infinite spirit that is One with an undivided *ousia*, or essence. The Father, Son, and Spirit are all of the same *ousia* (*homoousia*) but God has distinct instances of a given essence. Each person of God is *relationally distinct*, but they have a mutually interpenetrating unity, or what is often referred to as *perichoresis*, a type of divine dance with interlocking partners. Allow me to break all this down and make it very plain.

So, the Trinity is One God. Deuteronomy 6:4-5 says, "Hear, O Israel! The LORD is our God, the LORD is one!" Also, Deuteronomy 4:35 says, "To you it was shown that you might know that the LORD, He is God; there is no other besides Him." Isaiah 43:10 says, "You are My witnesses," declares the LORD, "And My servant whom I have chosen, so that you may know and believe Me and understand that I am He. Before Me there was no God formed, and there will be none after Me." I Timothy 2:5 says, "For there is one God."

But aren't there other gods? Jesus says in John 17:3, "Father, the hour has come; glorify Your Son, that the Son may glorify You, even as You gave Him authority over all flesh, that to all whom You have given Him, He may give eternal life. This is eternal life, that they may know You, the only true God, and Jesus Christ whom You have sent." Deuteronomy 32:17 says, "They sacrificed to demons who were not God, to gods whom they have not known, new gods who came lately, whom your fathers did not dread." For millennia, people have been worshipping and sacrificing to false deities that are *not* supreme, that are *not* the One True God, that are *not* the Trinitarian God of the Bible. They are imposters.

So, what this means in practice is that Jesus is not the Father. The Holy Spirit is not the Son, and the Father is not the Holy Spirit (you get the idea). Yet all three are God!

The Father is God. John 6:27 says, "Do not work for the food which perishes, but for the food which endures to eternal life, which the Son of Man will give to you, for on Him the Father, God, has set His seal." I Corinthians 8:6 says, "Yet for us there is but one God, the Father, from whom are all things and we exist for Him; and one Lord, Jesus Christ, by whom are all things, and we exist through Him."

Jesus is God. In John 1 it says, "In the beginning was the Word, and the Word was with God, and the Word was God. He was in the beginning with God ... And the Word became flesh, and dwelt among us." The Word becoming flesh was Jesus, so "in the beginning" with the Father was Jesus (the Word), who is also God. In John 8:58 Jesus says, "Truly, truly, I say to you, before Abraham was born, I am." Referring to Himself as God, or "I am," is exactly the same way the Father referred to Himself as God in Exodus 3:14 when God said to Moses, "I AM WHO I AM"; and He said, "Thus you shall say to the sons of Israel, 'I AM has sent me to you.'" Titus 2:13 says, "looking for the blessed hope and the appearing of the glory of our great God and Savior, Christ Jesus." Hebrews 1:1-3 says that Jesus is the exact representation of God the Father: "God, after He spoke long ago to the fathers in the prophets in many portions and in many ways, in these last days has spoken to us in His Son, whom He appointed heir of all things, through whom also He made the world. And He is the radiance of His glory and the exact representation of His nature, and upholds all things by the word of His power." In John 14:9-11, Jesus said, "Don't you know me, Philip, even after I have been among you such a long time? Anyone who has seen me has seen the Father. How can you say, 'Show us the Father'? Don't you believe that I am in the Father, and that the Father is in me? The words I say to you I do not speak on my own authority. Rather, it is the Father, living in me, who is doing his work. Believe me when I say that I am in the Father and the Father is in me; or at least believe on the evidence of the works themselves."

The Holy Spirit is God. II Corinthians 3:17-18 says, "Now the Lord is the Spirit, and where the Spirit of the Lord is, there is liberty. But we all, with unveiled face, beholding as in a mirror the glory of the Lord, are being transformed into the same image from glory to glory, just as from the Lord, the Spirit." Acts 5:3-4 reads, "But Peter said, 'Ananias, why has Satan filled your heart to lie to the Holy Spirit and to keep back some of the price of the land? While it remained unsold, did it not remain your own? And after it was sold, was it not under your control? Why is it that you have conceived this deed in your heart? You have not lied to men but to God.'" In Psalm 139:7, David equates God's omnipresence with the Holy Spirit: "Where can I go from Your Spirit? Or where can I flee from Your presence? If I ascend to Heaven, You are there; If I make my bed in Sheol, behold, You are there."

Notably, the Holy Spirit is not an impersonal "It." For example, in Ephesians 4:30 it says, "Do not grieve the Holy Spirit of God, by whom you were sealed for the day of redemption." The Spirit can be resisted: "You men who are stiff-necked and uncircumcised in heart and ears are always resisting the Holy

Spirit; you are doing just as your fathers did" (Acts 7:51). Hebrews 10:29 says, "How much severer punishment do you think he will deserve who has trampled underfoot the Son of God, and has regarded as unclean the blood of the covenant by which he was sanctified, and has insulted the Spirit of grace?"

The Holy Spirit is not only the Spirit of truth,[51] but also the teacher of that truth to believers,[52] and dwells within those believers.[53] In other words, true awareness, knowledge, and understanding of God comes directly from God, and thus, God will never reveal non-truth about Himself to anyone. By implication then, anyone who proclaims something as truth that is contradictory to the Word of God in the Scriptures is not revealing truth at all, but false doctrine. The Holy Spirit, being God with full and complete understanding of the truth, *is incapable* of lying and teaching false doctrine. So, a person who believes that they can live a Christian life filled with what the Bible calls sin does not derive that belief from God.[54] Truth comes directly from God by the Holy Spirit and is therefore never derived from us or what we "feel" on the inside, but is external, objective, changeless, and timeless. We conform to the truth; the truth never, ever conforms to us.

I John 4:8 says, "The one who does not love does not know God, for God is love." Understanding the Trinity of God, then, means understanding love. Within the Trinity, there is relationship, friendship, harmony, unity, and happiness. The essence of the Trinity is love. John 3:35 says, "The Father loves the Son and has given all things into His hand." In John 14:31, Jesus says, "I love the Father, I do exactly as the Father commanded Me." Hence, you and I and everyone, all made in the image of God,[55] were made *from* love *with* love *to* love and *to be* loved, but in order to properly understand and execute this, we need God, which is where our conception of love started.

---

[51] John 14:17; 1 John 4:6
[52] John 14:26, 15:26, 16:12-15; 1 John 2:20, 26-27
[53] Romans 5:5, 8:9; 14-16; 1 Corinthians 3:16; Ephesians 1:13-14; 1 John 4:13
[54] Titus 1:16; 1 John 1:8, 10, 2:3-6, 9-11, 3:6-11, 4:20-21
[55] Genesis 1:27

What Christians should know is that the distinction of God's persons is important because there is an *imminent* and an *economic* Trinity. The imminent Trinity refers to how God relates to Himself. The economic Trinity refers to how God works in history in order to accomplish various tasks. So, the different persons of the Trinity are distinct as a function of their *relation to each other and the world*. It follows, then, that the Father, Son, and Spirit are the same, and they are made distinct by their relations. So, to Himself God is all the same and imminently works in perfect harmony and unison, but in regard to the salvation of humanity, for example, each person of the Trinity plays a different role to accomplish a task. For example, I Peter 1:2 says, "According to the foreknowledge of God the Father, by the sanctifying work of the Spirit, to obey Jesus Christ and be sprinkled with His blood: May grace and peace be yours in the fullest measure." In other words, God the Father knew beforehand whom He would save. God the Son came into this world in order to live, die, and be resurrected, and God the Spirit works in and through us to empower us in the Christian path, so that we can be reconciled back to the Father through Christ. Our whole salvation is Trinitarian.[56]

Here's another way of looking at it. God the Father speaks a word in Heaven. Jesus, the Son, is the Word of God[57] that became flesh[58] and lived with us for a few decades on Earth. After His death and resurrection, Jesus ascended to Heaven[59] after paying the ultimate price for sin,[60] thus creating a new spiritual bridge between the Father and us. (This is why Jesus is so critically important, because without the divine sacrifice salvation would be impossible). Soon after Jesus went up to Heaven, the Holy Spirit came down (Pentecost), subsequently empowering us to

---

[56] Ephesians 1:3-14
[57] John 1:1
[58] John 1:14
[59] Luke 24:51
[60] Romans 6:23; I John 4:10

manifest the fruits of an obedient life,[61] so that we may one day cross the bridge back to the Father.

Here are some more examples of the economic Trinity. God the Father spoke the universe into existence in Genesis 1, and in John 1:3 it says the Father acted *through* Jesus: "All things came into being through Him, and apart from Him nothing came into being that has come into being."

The Father is the One who sent Jesus into the world[62] and planned for the redemption of humankind.[63] It is the foreknowledge of the Father that allows only Him to predestine those who will believe and follow Christ.[64]

The Father does not advocate for us before Himself—only Jesus does. This is why I John 2:1 says, "If anyone sins, we have an Advocate with the Father, Jesus Christ the righteous." Christ is the perfect divine mediator. Hence, Hebrews 7:25 says, "Therefore He is able to save forever those who draw near to God through Him, since He always lives to make intercession for them." Notably, *only Jesus,* Incarnated as Man, was rejected by many, suffered and died on a cross, and then was resurrected three days later. Neither the Father nor the Holy Spirit died on a cross.

The Holy Spirit is called a Helper, a distinction apart from the Father and Jesus: "But the Helper,[65] the Holy Spirit, whom the Father will send in My name, He will teach you all things, and bring to your remembrance all that I said to you."[66] Romans 8:27 says, "He who searches the hearts knows what the mind of the Spirit is, because He intercedes for the saints according to the will of God." In John 16:7, Jesus says, "But I tell you the truth, it is to your advantage that I go away; for if I do not go away the Helper will not come to you; but if I go, I will send Him to you."

---

[61] Galatians 5:22-23
[62] John 3:16
[63] Galatians 4:4; Ephesians 1:9-10
[64] Romans 8:29; 1 Peter 1:2
[65] In Greek *parakletos,* a term meaning one who pleads a case before a judge, a comforter, advocate, intercessor, or legal assistant.
[66] John 14:26

The Holy Spirit is also described as distributing gifts,[67] gifting speech,[68] and interceding.[69] It is a unique attribute of the Spirit that regenerates us to give us new, invigorated, spiritual lives,[70] and to empower us.[71]

A fancy way of describing the Trinitarian dynamic is "ontological equality but economic subordination." Or put more simply, "of the same stuff, but willingly submitting in order to do a job." To be clear, no member of the Trinity is subordinate, inferior, or non-equal to the other two, but there is deference or voluntary *subordination of will* without ontological subordination. Accordingly, as Wayne Grudem says, "If we do not have ontological equality, not all the persons are fully God. But if we do not have economic subordination, then there is no inherent difference in the way the three persons relate to one another."[72]

Without question, there is explicit reference to the Trinity in the New Testament, and there are also many implications of it in the Old. For example, in Genesis 1:1 it says, "In the beginning God …" Here, the word God (*elohim* in Hebrew) is plural, yet words conjoined to this verb in Hebrew grammar are singular so God (plural) *is* and not are. There is a form of speech in Hebrew grammar called "plural of majesty" where referring to a single person in the plural denotes respect, but this method is not used in any other place in the Old Testament. Verse 1 goes on to say, "… and *the Spirit of God* was moving over the surface of the waters" (italics are mine). In verse 2, God famously says, "Let there be light," and light is often used in reference to Jesus, the Son, when he refers to Himself, as in, "I am the light of the world"[73] and "While I am in the world, I am the Light of the world."[74] So, within the first few verses of the Bible, we are

---

[67] I Corinthians 12:11
[68] Acts 8:29
[69] Romans 8:26-27
[70] John 3:5-8
[71] Acts 1:8; 1 Corinthians 12:7-11
[72] Wayne Grudem, *Systematic Theology: An Introduction to Biblical Doctrine* (Grand Rapids: Zondervan, 1994), 251.
[73] John 8:12
[74] John 8:5

introduced to the Trinity at work before the world as we know it was born.

Furthermore, Genesis 1:26 says, "Then God said, 'Let *Us* make man in *Our* image, according to *Our* likeness'" (italics mine). Genesis 3:22 says, "Behold, the man has become like one of *Us*." The Psalmist refers to more than one person as God in two places: Psalm 45:6-7, "Therefore God, Your God ..."; and Psalm 110:1, where David says, "The LORD says to my Lord; 'Sit at My right hand until I make Your enemies a footstool for Your feet.'" The first passage is referred to in Hebrews (1:8) but is specifically applied to Christ. The implication of the second passage is that: (A) David is calling two distinct persons Lord; and (B) The LORD could only make God sit at His right hand.

Isaiah 61:1 says, "The Spirit of the Lord God is upon me." The implication is that the Spirit and the Lord God are distinct. Isaiah 63:10 says, "But they rebelled and grieved His Holy Spirit." All three members of the Trinity are mentioned in Isaiah 48:16, where the speaker says, "And now the LORD GOD has sent Me, and His Spirit." The speaker, presumably the Son, mentions being sent as well as the Spirit. In Luke 4, Jesus reads a scroll that has Isaiah 61 written on it, and then in 4:21 says, "Today this Scripture has been fulfilled in your hearing."

The clearest representation of all three persons of the Trinity at once occurs at the baptism of Jesus. Matthew 3:16-17 says, "After being baptized, Jesus came up immediately from the water; and behold, the heavens were opened, and he saw the Spirit of God descending as a dove and lighting on Him, and behold, a voice out of the heavens said, 'This is My beloved Son, in whom I am well pleased.'" Here, simultaneously, all three members of the Trinity perform a different function: the Father speaks, the Son is baptized, and the Spirit descends to anoint for ministry.

In Matthew 28:19, Christ tells the disciples, "Go therefore and make disciples of all the nations, baptizing them in the name of the Father, and the Son and the Holy Spirit." Jude 1:20-21 says, "But you, beloved, building yourselves up on your most holy faith, praying in the Holy Spirit, keep yourselves in the love of

God, waiting anxiously for the mercy of our Lord Jesus Christ to eternal life."

A proper understanding of the Trinity changes the very way a Christian thinks about life itself, because the Trinity is a relational dynamic, and we, as Christians, are in a relationship with God. The Trinitarian God of the Bible is One already in a relationship with Himself before the creation of the world. As a result, love, which is other-dependent, existed *before* God exerted His power. This distinguishes God as One already in love and fellowship with another before creation from other impersonal unitarian gods who needed to create in order to enter into a relationship. The entire doctrine of salvation is based solely on the Trinity, without which we could not be saved, and through these relationships, we are reconciled back to God—that is, *by* the Holy Spirit working in us, *through* Jesus Christ, back *to* the Father in Heaven.

This reveals that the human experience is intended to be loving and communal; hence, it is not good for individuals to be alone[75] because our lives are meant to be community-oriented, simply because that's who God is, and we are all made in His image. Furthermore, all three persons of the Trinity are fully transparent, honest, good, and truthful, and this provides a blueprint of how we should live. God is One all the time, without variance and without change, which means His character never changes based on circumstances. He pours out His love and shares His eternal attributes freely and openly, without bounds. There is giving without ceasing and also humility because Jesus, being fully God, voluntarily subjugated Himself for our sake.[76] He redefined power, then, not by using it against us but by emptying Himself for us. Hence, not "My will be done, but your will"[77] and "When you lose your life is when you really find it."[78] Truly, Jesus, being fully God, submitted to the Father out of love. As a result, there is love without argument, lying, poor communica-

---

[75] Genesis 2:18
[76] Philippians 2:5-8
[77] Luke 22:42
[78] Matthew 10:39

tion, disrespect, criticism, or covetousness. In the context of relationship, Jesus knew the Father was equal, but He submitted and obeyed. This reorganizes any misconceptions or pollution from American ideology about how a Christian ought to act in marriages, institutions, friendships, churches, and communities, and honoring one's mother and father. An ideology that says otherwise, that uses power *for the sake of self*, as in "I am right," "I will not respect those in authority because I am better," or "They're beneath me" is inconsistent with the Trinity and consistent with the world.

What Christians should know is that there have been many heresies regarding the doctrine of the Trinity. Even small deviations put you on a path where you end up way off course. There are three main false doctrines.

(1) God is not One, but many. This is essentially polytheism. Another fallacy is Tritheism, which says that God is three and not One.

(2) God is not three persons, or He's *one* actor with three different masks—modalism, for example, says that God remains the same person but changes his face mask depending on what scene of the play is happening on stage. The obvious problem with this ideology can be found in passages like Matthew 3 that show God simultaneously being Father, Spirit (dove), and Son *at the same time.* In the Garden of Gethsemane (Luke 22:39-46), Jesus prays to the Father in Heaven, making the modalism hypothesis impossible.

(3) Claiming that any member of the Trinity is not equally God. Arianism was a heretical doctrine that was resolved at the Council of Nicea in 325 A.D. Arius, a bishop in the Alexandrian Church, said that Jesus was not God, and was at some point in history created by God the Father. Adoptionism, or the idea that God "adopted" Jesus at some point, thereby making a fully human male His son, is also

heretical. For clarity on this matter, please refer to the paragraphs above.

What Christians should know is that God has multiple names, and each pertains to a specific aspect of His deity.

Yahweh is the proper name for God and is what God chose as a label for Himself in Exodus 3:14 when he said, "I AM WHO I AM." This name emphasizes the covenantal relationship that God has with His people. Jehovah can also be used to express the same meaning, or "the existing One." Elohim is first used in Genesis 1:1, and this name emphasizes God as supreme over everything, including other false gods. Adonai means "the Lord God" or "Lord of the whole Earth."

The name of God incarnate, Jesus, means "the Savior of Mankind." The English word Christ comes from the Greek word *Christos*, which means Messiah or anointed. Thus, when someone says "Jesus Christ," they are literally saying, "The Savior of Mankind, the Messiah."

Compound names are also used to describe specific characteristics. For example, Jehovah Jirah means, "the Lord will provide," as used in Genesis 22:13-14. El-Shaddai ("El," the root from "Elohim") means "God Almighty" and emphasizes the LORD'S power.

Names in our world are usually easily explicable: typically, our parents gave them to us, often for specific reasons. There is, however, only one explanation for the name of God in the Hebrew Bible, and it comes from Exodus 3:14-15. There it says, "God said to Moses, 'I AM WHO I AM,'" and He said, "Thus you shall say to the sons of Israel, 'I AM has sent me to you.'" Furthermore, God said to Moses, "Thus you shall say to the sons of Israel, 'The LORD, the God of your fathers, the God of Abraham, the God of Isaac, and the God of Jacob, has sent me to you.' This is my name forever, and this is My memorial name to all generations." The Hebrew root of "I AM" is *'ehyeh* (Yahweh). Furthermore, in this statement, God connects His name to the Elohim of Israel's fathers. In other words, "Yahweh, the Elohim of your fathers, the Elohim of Abraham, the Elohim of Isaac, and the Elohim of Jacob, has sent me to you."[79] Gottwald says, "Exodus 3:14 regards the divine name as formed from the Hebrew verb *hyh*, 'to be.'" If this verb is understood in this simple stem, *'ehyeh* means 'I will be' or 'I am,' and Yahweh is understood to mean 'he will be' or 'he (always) is.'" The Greek translation of the Old Testament renders *'ehyeh* into "I am the one who (eternally) is."[80]

What Christians should know and now realize is that the Trinitarian God of the Bible is complex, thought-provoking, and is in no way "simple," or "easily mastered." So, the many people in the world who dismiss Christianity as a refuge for the ignorant or a consolation to the intellectually challenged truly reveal that they have no idea of who God is, nor have they ever taken the time to understand sound doctrine. Getting a firm grasp on the Trinity requires earnest effort and discipline on the part of the believer. So if you feel as if you haven't gotten it yet, do not be discouraged, that's the normal response! It took one of the greatest theologians in history (Augustine) more than a decade to complete his analysis of the Trinity.

For Further Study

Saint Augustine and Edmond Hill, *The Trinity*, ed. John E. Rotelle (Hyde Park: New City Press, 2012). Augustine's theological work on the Trinity has stood the test of time even though it was written more than 1,500 years ago. If you want a good place to start, start here.

Wayne Grudem, *Systematic Theology: An Introduction to Biblical Doctrine* (Grand Rapids: Zondervan, 1994). A sound guide to Biblical doctrine that will assist any diligent Bible student in their search to know and understand.

---

[79] Norman K. Gottwald, *The Hebrew Bible: A Brief Socio-Literary Introduction* (Minneapolis: Fortress Press, 2009), 120.
[80] Ibid, 120.

CHAPTER III
THE BIBLE

Before I dive into the chapter, I'd like to take a moment to focus your attention on where we're going. People often think the Bible is not relevant to their lives, is out of touch, or perceive it as something too big or complicated to grasp. It's a problem of expectation because people either suppose something the Bible isn't (for example, a roadmap to a stress-free life), or assume little to nothing about it because they fail to realize what the Bible really is.

What Christians should know is that the Bible offers a new way of looking at and understanding the world. This fresh perspective ultimately leads to life, peace, joy, and the completeness so many are searching for.

The Bible awakens a dormant imagination within all of us; this consciously and unconsciously forms our identity and, therefore, determines how we perceive and interact with the world.

Walter Brueggemann labels the Biblical example a *covenantal-historical model* of contemplating our existence and our faith in God. This model implies "an enduring commitment between God and God's people based on mutual vows of loyalty and mutual obligation through which both parties have their life radically affected and empowered."[81] As a result, the meaning of our lives is not rooted in ourselves so that we just get out what we put in. Rather, there is Someone greater than us all, and through grace, despite what we "having coming to us," God trusts in and takes humanity so seriously that in spite of our depravity because of sin, we can all be saved. The Word of God

---

[81] Walter Brueggemann, *The Bible Makes Sense* (Cincinnati: St. Anthony Messenger Press, 2003), 10.

reveals there is something timeless, better, and more powerful than what this world has to offer. The Bible gives everyone a genuine, fresh identity that refuses to allow us to forget who we truly are, demands obedience to expectations, and will not allow us to settle for the false identities the world would have us adopt.

The Bible is much more than a good idea or an ideology that has an alternative end. It is a concrete and unchanging fixed point of reference in an ever-changing world characterized by identity crises, displacement, and burden. From that fixed identity, we derive our life's mission and calling. The Bible locates us in fellowship with God and therefore in fellowship with other servants of God. Thus, we all belong to a community of believers and all have a responsible and caring family in one another—we are, therefore, not all alone and have definite meaning and purpose in each other *through Christ*. The Bible teaches us that we all have a unique prospect for the future where those in the front will be in the back and those on the bottom will be on top.

As Walter Brueggemann so eloquently says in *The Bible Makes Sense*, "The Bible provides us with an alternative identity, an alternative way of understanding ourselves, an alternative way of relating to the world. It offers a radical and uncompromising challenge to our ordinary ways of self-understanding. It invites us to join in and to participate in the ongoing pilgrimage of those who live in the sharing of history ... The surprises of the resurrection concern the emergence of expected new life in persons, in institutions, in social arrangements. And they come just when we think there are no more reasonable expectations."[82]

The Bible teaches us that when the world says "No" God says "Yes." The Bible teaches us that when the world says, "You're not" God says, "I AM." The Bible teaches us that when you thought you were destined to be enslaved to death, Christ sets you free to live.

---

[82] Ibid, 20-21.

I. What is the Bible?

The Bible is the Word of God. It is pure,[83] perfect,[84] and true;[85] it is the perfect guide for our lives,[86] nourishes us,[87] and is the lamp that guides us in the darkness.[88]

This Word is a person, Jesus (John 1). The Word is God's speech, for example, when God decrees, "Let there be light" (Gen 1:3).

The Word is a personal address to a group of people or to an individual, as seen when God comes down and speaks to Israel gathered at Mount Sinai in Exodus 20. Another example is seen when God speaks from heaven at the baptism of Jesus and says, "This is My beloved Son, in whom I am well-pleased" (Matthew 3:17).

The Word is speech through a human vehicle. Deuteronomy 18:18 says, "I will raise up a prophet from among their countrymen like you, and *I will put My words in his mouth*, and he shall speak to them all that I command him" (emphasis added).

The Word is in written form to preserve it accurately: anyone can refer back to it and inspect it, study it, recite it, use it, and apply it. The written word also makes the Bible accessible to anyone who wishes to read it. In Exodus 31:18, God wrote the Ten Commandments on stone tablets Himself before giving the tablets to Moses: "When He had finished speaking with him upon Mount Sinai, He gave Moses the two tablets of the testimony, tablets of stone, *written by the finger of God*" (italics mine). In other instances, people inscribed what God told them. Moses wrote down additional laws God gave him.[89] Other examples of people writing down and inscribing what God had told them include Joshua,[90] Isaiah,[91] and Jeremiah.[92] The Holy Spirit

---

[83] Psalm 119:140
[84] Psalm 19:7
[85] Psalm 119:160
[86] Proverbs 6:23
[87] Jeremiah 15:16
[88] Psalm 119:150
[89] Deuteronomy 31:9-13, 24-26
[90] Joshua 24:26
[91] Isaiah 30:8

brought remembrance of Christ's words to the disciples so they could faithfully remember and record what Jesus told them.[93] In his letter to the church at Corinth, the apostle Paul wrote, "the things which I write to you are the Lord's commandment" (I Corinthians 14:37).

The word Bible derives from the Greek work *biblia*, or book. Essentially, God wrote it by revealing it to human authors (about 40) who faithfully recorded what the Holy Spirit inspired them to write. The words are God's but the vehicle used to transcribe those words is a select group of humans. This process of divine revelation for Biblical transcription is called *verbal plenary inspiration*.[94] (Note that this term, like "Trinity" is a human construction intended to describe a Biblical phenomenon. The word does *not* appear in the Bible). II Peter 1:20-21 says, "But know this first of all, that no prophecy of Scripture is a matter of one's own interpretation, for no prophecy was ever made by an act of human will, but men moved by the Holy Spirit spoke from God." In addition, because God is truth,[95] He inspired the authors to write what is wholly true.[96]

The Bible is more than a mere book because the Holy Scriptures pre-existed their physical and tangible forms. In essence, the Word of God is eternal and timeless without equal in the realm of human existence. At the start of John's gospel, the text reads, "In the beginning was the Word, and the Word was with God, and the Word was God. He was in the beginning with God. All things came into being through Him, and apart from Him nothing came into being that has come into being." Further on, in 1:14, it reads, "And the Word became flesh, and dwelt among us, and we saw His glory as of the only begotten from the Father, full of grace and truth." "The Word became flesh" refers to Christ. Therefore, in the same way God is timeless and eternal, so is His

---

[92] Jeremiah 30:2, 36:2-4
[93] John 14:26
[94] II Timothy 3:16-17, Exodus 20:1-17, I Kings 12:22-24, I Chronicles 17:3-4, Jeremiah 35:13, Ezekiel 2:4-7, Zechariah 7:9-10, II Corinthians 5:20, II Peter 1:20-21
[95] Psalm 116:160, John 17:17, Ephesians 1:13-14, Titus 1:2, James 1:18, Hebrews 6:18
[96] I Corinthians 2:12-13, II Timothy 3:16-17, I Peter 1:10-12

Word; and if His Word transcends our existence, we ought to pay full attention and listen to what God wants us to hear.

Hebrews 4:12 speaks of the Word as "living and active and sharper than any two-edged sword, and piercing as far as the division of soul and spirit." Certainly, when God repeats or reiterates a message, we have to pay special attention.

The Bible has 66 books (39 in the Old Testament and 27 in the New Testament). The Old Testament (OT) takes us from creation to a time before the coming of Christ, and the New Testament (NT) begins with the birth (0 AD), life, death, and resurrection of Christ. In fact, the first four chapters of the NT are four different perspectives of Jesus, including details about the things He did and the things He said. The NT continues by giving Christians and Christian churches instructions on how to think, live, and act appropriately.

The OT makes up the overwhelming majority (more than 75 percent) of the entire Bible. In fact, the OT has 929 chapters and 23,214 verses. The NT has 260 chapters and 7,959 verses. Keep in mind that the chapters and verses in the Bible are human constructs added in the second millennium simply for organizational purposes. The original writings of the OT were written on papyrus, an old form of paper that often consisted of long scrolls. The original writings of the NT were written on parchment, or specially prepared animal skins. The OT spans a history of thousands of years and the NT spans a history of less than 100 years. The OT is written in Hebrew (some small parts are written in Aramaic) and the NT is written in Greek.

One way to think about the OT is that it describes how God initiated and developed a relationship with humanity. It began with individuals, and then grew into a much larger family and later an entire nation of people. The OT describes a God who establishes a series of covenants with a people who, despite all His warnings, fail to follow directions, which results in adverse consequences. Hence, because the people failed to follow commands and were incapable of obedience, a 'new way' had to exist. That 'new way' is described in the NT, with Jesus.

The Old Testament is revealed in the New Testament, and the NT is concealed in the Old. To understand truly the NT, one must first read the OT, as the NT is essentially a fulfillment of what was said before.

What Christians should know is that the Bible, above everything else, serves as a *theological statement* with a primary aim of revealing exactly Who God is, what He has done, and how we, as God's servants, are to engage in a relationship with Him.

Thus, while the Bible (or the Scriptures) does proceed through historical events with different people and places, its goal is always to give us *theological* meaning through the context of human history. If you need an exact play-by-play of how the universe went from this to that, you will *not* find it in the Bible, *nor does it claim to provide that information*. If you need to know how the power of Christ's atoning sacrifice frees you from the grip of sin, you're in the right place. The Bible contains authoritative truth, but non-contradictory truth can be found elsewhere.

Two Latin slogans summarize this idea. *Sola Scriptura* ("by Scripture alone") means the Scriptures alone are the highest form of authority. The phrase *prima Scriptura* means there are sources secondary to the Scriptures that allow us to know and understand God better, or guides we can follow, but these guides ultimately are judged and tested by the Scriptures. An example of such guides would be revelation through creation[97] or our consciences.[98] Therefore, the Bible is *the ultimate* source of truth by which all other sources are judged, *but not the only* source of truth. This is why I don't open a Bible if I need to figure out what antibiotic to use to treat a complicated skin infection.

For this reason, when we judge the Bible, we first have to ask ourselves what the book claims to present. Hence, the Bible seemingly lacking a piece of data does not tarnish its reputation. If I need help with my taxes, I don't open a book on home improvement, nor does this query negate the authority of the latter. If you

---

[97] Psalm 19:1
[98] Isaiah 30:19-22, Hebrews 9:14

consult the Bible with a tax question, you won't find a direct answer, but it will say that God gives humanity intellect and wisdom,[99] and those attributes, being from God and therefore good, can be used to seek and discover other forms of truth.

II. How can I trust the Bible?

The simplest answer for why you should trust the Bible is because it is the Word of God. The fundamental scripture verse that validates the authority of the Bible comes from II Timothy 3:16-17: "All Scripture is inspired by God and profitable for teaching, for reproof, for correction, for training in righteousness; so that the man of God may be adequate, equipped for every good work." In the book of John, Jesus said, "Scripture cannot be broken."[100]

All the OT prophets recorded what God directly told them, either by themselves[101] or through a scribe.[102] The frequent and repetitive use of the phrase "Thus says The LORD"[103] is an example of such revelation. As mentioned previously, the apostle Peter said that in regards to all the OT, "No prophecy of Scripture is a matter of one's own interpretation, for no prophecy was ever made by an act of human will, but men moved by the Holy Spirit spoke from God."[104]

The Bible, or the Word of God, is tested and tried,[105] and something that is timeless,[106] meaning it is as applicable then as it is now and as it will be in future. The Word can be trusted because it is more than a book; it's a viable, living organism whose trustworthiness is evidenced by the fact that it changes the person who reads it.[107] Because the Bible is complete and

---

[99] Daniel 1:17
[100] John 10:35
[101] Joshua 24:26, Isaiah 30:8, Ezekiel 43:11, Daniel 7:1-2
[102] Exodus 17:14, 34:28
[103] Jeremiah 22:1
[104] II Peter 1:20-21
[105] Psalm 18:30, Proverbs 30:5
[106] Isaiah 40:8
[107] Hebrews 4:12

everlasting, it specifically says that Jesus is the final word of God revealed to humanity,[108] no other books are to be written after the Bible's final book, Revelation,[109] and we will all experience Scriptural silence until the second coming of Christ.[110] Finally, nothing is to be added to the Bible.[111]

In practical terms, this means the Bible is complete, and anyone proclaiming to have something new to add to the Scriptures after the Scriptures were finished is a heretic who contradicts the Bible itself. If 'god' allegedly revealed himself to someone and directed them toward new 'scripture,' or if a divine messenger revealed new scripture for recital, then both instances are blatant fabrications contradictory to the Word of God.

Here is a very valid question: if human beings "wrote" the Bible, then why should I believe it's the inspired Word of God and not some fabricated human concoction?

There are actually four ways to answer this question. The first three look around from the inside and help to formalize a Christian's belief using what he or she has already discovered to be true. The last method looks around from the outside and is purely objective. It not only validates Christianity's truth claims but can also help the reader disprove many of the so-called "truth" claims of other religions.

(1) The first is to believe the repeated declarations of the Scriptures themselves to be the infallible Word of God, as already mentioned. The *authority* of Scripture pertains to the fact that all of the words in the Bible are God's words, so to obey those words means you obey God; to disobey those words means you disobey God. Because the Bible is *the* ultimate authority, it claims its supreme authority by its own words because no other authority can exceed it. Moreover, the Bible is *self-attesting* because if it needed to appeal to a higher authority for validation, it could not be *the* ultimate authority.

---

[108] Hebrews 1:1-2
[109] Revelation 22:18-19
[110] Revelation 22:20-21
[111] Deuteronomy 4:2, 12:32; Proverbs 30:5-6

(This debunks the fallacy that Biblical authority is a circular argument: we believe the Bible *is* the Word of God *because it claims to be* the Word of God, and those words come from God Himself. Of course I believe it's true, because it's God Who said it! In the same way, circular arguments are used all the time in the world but are perfectly legitimate. For example, how do you know you are reading these words? Because you're using your eyes, of course! However, do you not use your eyes to validate what your eyes see? So how do you know it's there if only *your* eyes see it?)

Thus, when God spoke through a prophet,[112] the human being was being used as a mouthpiece for The LORD Himself. The Bible's authority is also evidenced in the fact that the Bible has the power to change people for the better, and the Holy Spirit moves people when reading its words.[113] Since God cannot lie,[114] all of Scripture is refined, tested, true,[115] and is not only truthful but truth itself.[116] It is impossible for God to lie.[117] Hence, the Bible is *inerrant*, which means it is incapable of being wrong. The denial of inerrancy stems from one of the most dangerous phenomena in our modern world—the rejection of an ultimate, absolute truth in favor of a truth judged to be real only by personal experience.

Furthermore, the Bible has *clarity,* which means that anyone who earnestly seeks to know and understand God's teachings will be able to follow the Scriptures. In fact, even children can understand the Bible,[118] and it imparts understanding to the simple.[119] Yet, this does not dismiss the fact that some passages of the book are indeed difficult to understand.[120] The reader should be aware, however, that since the Bible is the incarnate

---

[112] Num. 22:38; Deut. 18:18-20; Ezek. 13:1-16; I Kings 14:18; Zech. 7:7
[113] I Corinthians 2:13-14
[114] Titus 1:2
[115] Psalm 12:6
[116] John 17:17
[117] Hebrews 6:18
[118] Deuteronomy 6:6-7
[119] Psalm 119:130
[120] II Peter 3:15-16

Word of God, it requires an open heart and mind to receive the gifts of the book; of course, someone with a closed heart will never be able to fully embrace the Word.[121] The Bible is also *necessary* because without it, we would not know about God, Jesus, faith, salvation, grace, sin, the prophets, the covenants, the gospel, or all the other wonderful things contained within it.

This is why in Romans 10:13-17, Paul says, "For 'Whoever will call on the name of the Lord will be saved.' How then will they call on Him in whom they have not believed? How will they believe in Him whom they have not heard? And how will they hear without a preacher? How will they preach unless they are sent? Just as it is written, 'How beautiful are the feet of those who bring good news of good things!' However, they did not all heed the good news; for Isaiah says, 'Lord, who has believed our report?' So faith *comes* from hearing, and hearing *by the word of Christ*" (italics mine). Thus, it is *necessary* to read the Bible to obtain knowledge of the gospel, maintain a spiritual life, and obtain knowledge of God's will to live a life that is more Christ-like.

The Bible is also *sufficient* meaning in that it contains everything God wanted us to know. In other words, we don't need anything else besides the Bible to be saved, trust in Him, and live a life of obedience.[122] This doesn't mean God can't add to His words; it means *we* can't. In the time after Moses's death, for example, all Israel had was five books (Genesis, Exodus, Leviticus, Numbers, and Deuteronomy). That was sufficient for them *at that time*, and God added to it over time, stopping by the end of the first century. The sufficiency of the Bible is a very important concept for our modern time because it means that *any* problem or question we have has an answer in the Bible. The answer may not be specific to your question, but the timeless Biblical principles satisfy all queries.

(2) The second answer attempts to determine what possible malicious and unifying reason any Biblical writer would have to

---

[121] I Corinthians 2:14, Hebrews 5:14
[122] II Timothy 3:15-16

fabricate a story *to his own detriment*. Moses, for example, who wrote the Bible's first five books, could have stayed in Egypt and lived the high life as a member of privileged society. However, he believed in a God that led him out of Egypt into a less-than-privileged life, to lead hundreds of thousands of grumblers and complainers in the desert for 40 years, to die before he arrived where he wanted to go. If all the apostles of the New Testament were fabricating a grand scheme, why did they deceive and what did they gain? All the apostles lived lives of ridicule and were killed mercilessly and prematurely. Peter, for example, was crucified upside down. To top it all off, the apostles died for the truth—all they had to do was recant, but they didn't. All Jesus had to do was say, "I am *not* God" and He would have been left alone, but He never recanted.

(3) In contrast to any other religious authority, the Bible describes people from many different times and in different geographic areas making and fulfilling prophecies all pointing in the same unified direction. It would be easy, for example, for me to state that I went up a mountain, into a cave, or to a field and received 'divine revelation' when I am the only barometer for my experience. But if multiple people unconnected to one another received the same revelation that not only reinforced what others heard but also accurately predicted what would happen hundreds of years in the future and the cost of declaring that word was death, separation from society, ridicule, and anguish, you have to begin paying attention.

There is an internal consistency in that the books of the Bible refer to themselves and other books as authoritative.[123] Jesus repeatedly referred to the OT Scriptures as authoritative and quoted many of them.[124] Also, the Bible repeatedly describes the fulfillment of prophecies often made hundreds of years earlier. For example, David prophesized that Jesus would be crucified hundreds of years before crucifixion existed.[125] More

---

[123] Joshua 1:8, Daniel 9:2, Ezekiel 14:14, 1 Corinthians 14:37, I Thessalonians 2:13, II Peter 3:15-16, Revelation 1:3
[124] Matthew 23:25; Luke 11:51, 24:44
[125] Psalm 22:16, Luke 23:33

than 500 years before Jesus was born, both David and Isaiah prophesized that Jesus would resurrect from the dead.[126] In addition, hundreds of years before the events came to fulfillment, Zechariah stated that Jesus would be betrayed for thirty pieces of silver,[127] Isaiah said Jesus's mother would be a virgin,[128] Micah said Jesus would be born in Bethlehem,[129] Hosea said Jesus's family would flee to Egypt,[130] and Malachi predicted that Jesus would enter the temple in Jerusalem.[131]

(4) The fourth approach is both historic and academic. A large chunk of this material is derived from Craig A. Parton's *Religion On Trial*, which is a marvelous book on how to objectively evaluate the validity of different religious truth claims.

Many things can be simultaneously false, but they cannot be simultaneously true given the contradictory claims they make. There can only be one truth, and being able to answer the question, "What is true?" requires the ability to objectively test religious claims with a system that is not derived from the authority you are investigating. *Experience* does not determine truth because some people can, for example, have a "life-changing" and "religious" experience with enough Prozac. Faith *by itself* does not determine truth because it only becomes valid when *the object* of that faith is clarified. What we are left with are the facts, or the *"final arbiters or judges of all competing interpretations."*[132]

So, most religious *claims* are in fact hocus-pocus because they are not religious *truths*. Why are they not truths? *Because they can't be verified.* It is only Christianity—whose credibility stems from the *historical* events of Jesus's life and resurrection—that can indeed be legally confirmed. The truth claims of Christianity

---

[126] Psalm 16:10, Isaiah 53:10-12, Acts 2:25-32.
[127] Zechariah 11:12-13, Matthew 26:14-15
[128] Isaiah 7:14, Matthew 1:18-23
[129] Micah 5:2, Luke 2:1-7
[130] Hosea 11:1, Matthew 2:13-15
[131] Malachi 3:1, Luke 2:25-27
[132] Craig A. Parton, *Religion on Trial* (Eugene, OR: Wipf & Stock, 2008), 26.

are not only based upon verifiable facts, but those facts do not require pre-existing belief, they will never have 100% certainty (as is true for the present and history), and its truth remains regardless of whether or not people accept it as true.

In regards to gauging the reliability of the source document of the Bible, we have to look at four independent, first-hand eyewitness accounts at the beginning of the New Testament: the books of Matthew, Mark, Luke, and John. We will start here because these four books all detail the central truth claim of Christianity: the resurrection of Jesus Christ, who entered into reality being fully God and fully man (more on that in a later). Three tests will be applied: (1) The *bibliographical* test, which determines how reliably the ancient documents have been passed down (e.g., if an original manuscript exists, how many copies exist, and how large is the time gap between the event and the recording); (2) The *internal evidence* test, which explores what the text reveals about itself in order to gauge its reliability (e.g., is the author a first-hand eyewitness or did they have the skill to write about the actual events that occurred); (3) *The external evidence* test, which looks at information peripheral to the document and questions whether that information supports or refutes the document's claims. It is rare for ancient documents to have external confirmatory evidence.

In examining ancient secular writers (e.g., Plato, Homer, and Caesar), the bibliographical test reveals that, "much of what we know of the classical world is built upon the very thinnest of evidential or documentary trails."[133] However, "when we turn our attention to the writers of the four accounts of the life of Jesus Christ that are contained in the New Testament, the difference could not be greater. Even liberal and atheist biblical scholars agree that Matthew, Mark, Luke, and John are the best primary source recorders of the life of Jesus."[134] The point is this: using the same scale, if one were to reject the books of Matthew, Mark, Luke, and John as valid historical documents, then one

---

[133] Ibid, 48.
[134] Ibid, 49.

would also have to essentially reject the bulk of the entire canon of Western literature from Ancient Greece to the modern era (including Shakespeare). Application of the internal evidence test to the books of Matthew, Mark, Luke, and John reveals the following: "The consistent conclusion of legally trained trial lawyers over the last 300 years is that this material comes with the absolute best manuscript tradition possible, that it comes on top of the events that it records, that it is highly unlikely to have been forged, and that it contains the type of stylistic and factual detail you expect from truthful witnesses (i.e., liars love generalities while those telling the truth are not afraid of piling on historical particulars)."[135]

The external evidence test locates several non-Biblical historical works confirming both the claims made by writers of the books of the Bible and historical events referred to in the Bible. For example, Papias of Hieropolis (ca. 155) and Polycarp recorded what the apostle John told them directly and stated that the books of Matthew, Mark, Luke, and John were written by the authors ascribed to them.[136] Eusebius wrote that Paul and Peter died during the Neronian persecution,[137] and there is also archeological confirmation of Pilate's existence by the "Pilate Inscription" found in Jerusalem.

Also, numerous non-Biblical sources locate Jesus (and especially the historical event of the resurrection) and Christians in history. Examples include the writings of Seutonius, Pliny the Younger, and the Jewish historian Flavius Josephus, as well as accounts of early Christian martyrs who suffered and died at the hands of historical governments because of the reality of Christ and his resurrection. Several examples can be found in part one of *Readings in World Christian History* and include, for example, The Martyrdom of Perpetua and Felicity, The Martyrs of Lyons, and Ignatius's *Letters to the Magnesians*.

---

[135] Ibid, 57.
[136] Ibid, 58.
[137] Eusebius, *Historica ecclesiastica*, Book II, section 25.

I say all of this to make a very important point: the life, death, and resurrection of Jesus Christ is the central claim upon which the entire Christian faith is based. Without the resurrection, Christianity is null and void. Yet, the objective doubts that can be amassed against Matthew, Mark, Luke, and John illuminate the Bible's power to resist scrutiny. These books are verifiable based on multiple, independent, legitimate historical sources, and their contents not only pass the three tests, but their messages have real and relevant prescriptions that can change lives.

Trusting the Bible means trusting it in a physical, literal, and spiritual sense. This is why Jesus asked Nicodemus in John 3:12, "If I told you earthly things and you do not believe, how will you believe if I tell you heavenly things?" One cannot separate the facts of the Bible from its theology, morals, and teachings. For example, Adam cannot be 'just a myth' because then the doctrine of the inheritance of sin and the downfall of all of humankind is wrong.[138] If Jesus wasn't born of a virgin, then his birth would be no different from that of the rest of humanity; he would be predestined to sin and, therefore, unable to atone for humankind through His death. Christ literally hung on a cross, and his blood literally was shed, and His body literally died and rose again three days later. Without the shedding of blood, there could not be any remission of sin.[139]

III. How did the Bible assume its current form?

Wayne Grudem says it best: "[T]he ultimate criterion of canonicity is divine authorship, not human or ecclesiastical approval."[140]

The Biblical canon is the list of all the books that belong in the Bible. The process by which books were chosen is called *canonization. Canon* means 'measuring rod.'

---

[138] Romans 5:12
[139] Hebrews 9:22
[140] Wayne Grudem, *Systematic Theology: An Introduction to Biblical Doctrine* (Grand Rapids: Zondervan, 1994), 68.

The OT was written roughly between 1200 BC and the first few hundred years before the birth of Christ, predominantly in Hebrew (some parts were in Aramaic).[141] Although *written* in this time, the composition of the OT spanned thousands of years, and a tremendous oral tradition existed in ancient Jewish society prior to the written texts taking form. In fact, the Bible as we know it today began when God gave His first written laws—the Ten Commandments—on stone tablets directly to Moses to give to the people of Israel (Exodus 31:18). These tablets were regarded as special and authoritative, placed in a very special container (the Ark of the Covenant),[142] and without question were esteemed as the direct work and writing of God.[143] From there, Moses wrote the Bible's first five books,[144] and later other individuals, such as Joshua, Samuel, David, Solomon, and Isaiah, wrote the other books over time. The OT is the Bible Jesus used because the NT did not exist yet.

The OT books were not chosen randomly but fulfill specific criteria: (1) A prophet of The LORD wrote them.[145] (2) What those prophets said was consistent with what other prophets said.[146] (3) An act of God confirmed the authority of the prophet.[147] (4) What the prophets said carried the authority to influence lives.[148] (5) The community accepted the prophetic utterings as true.[149]

After about 435 BC, there were no further additions to the OT canon. However, within the Apocrypha are books composed after 435 BC. The Jewish community never accepted these books as scripture, and they are not included in the Hebrew Bible (our OT with some organizational differences). They contain some

---

[141] Norman K. Gottwald, *The Hebrew Bible: A Brief Socio-Literary Introduction* (Minneapolis: Fortress Press, 2009) 57.
[142] Deuteronomy 10:5
[143] Exodus 32:16
[144] Exodus 17:14, 24:4, 34:27; Numbers 33:2; Deuteronomy 31:22
[145] Deuteronomy 18:18-22
[146] Deuteronomy 13:1-5
[147] Hebrews 2:3-4
[148] Hebrews 4:12
[149] Daniel 9:2

speculation about the end of days, historical accounts, short stories, and advice on how to live life day-to-day. Once Jesus arrived on the scene and raised up disciples, He and the other authors of the New Testament cited the authoritative OT Scriptures more than 295 times,[150] *excluding* the Apocrypha and thus formalizing the exclusive validity of the OT. The Roman Catholic Church *does* include the Apocrypha in its Biblical canon even though the Apocrypha does not claim authority as the rest of the Scriptures do and despite that they proclaim as truth claims that are *inconsistent* with the rest of the Bible.

Historically speaking, Israel did not begin as a people that based its culture or religion on books until the end of the Biblical period. In addition, because Israel was a small yet distinct sociohistorical entity, the writers of the Bible's books never had any awareness they were writing an authoritative 'Bible' that would lay the groundwork for a religion. Instead, the OT writers were particularly concerned with communal need and Israelite crises.[151] Therefore, there really has never been any significant debate about what belonged in the Hebrew Bible, or the OT.

The NT is a different story. After Christ resurrected and ascended, Christianity was becoming a 'big deal' in ancient Roman society—after all, this guy called Jesus rose from the dead after being crucified by the powerful Romans and told everyone they could live with Him in heaven. Many apostles were eyewitnesses to Christ and His life, but the potential for fraud, abuse, and self-gain in writing an NT 'book' became apparent. Hence, the canon of the NT was chosen based on several criteria: (1) The authors of books based their writings on eyewitness testimony of the events in Christ's life.[152] (2) Christ's followers accepted them as legitimate, and they revealed how the power of God can change people's lives for the better.[153] (3)

---

[150] Roger Nicole, "New Testament Use of the Old Testament," in *Revelation and the Bible*, ed. Carl F. H. Henry (London: Tyndale Press, 1959), 137-41.
[151] Norman K. Gottwald, *The Hebrew Bible: A Brief Socio-Literary Introduction* (Minneapolis: Fortress Press, 2009) 57.
[152] John 19:35, II Peter 1:16
[153] Colossians 4:16, I Timothy 5:18, I Peter 3:16

What they said agreed with the rest of the Scriptures.[154]

There are exceptions to these rules. Luke, for example, wrote his two books (Luke and Acts) after receiving information from Paul,[155] and after both collecting information from a multitude of eyewitnesses and "having investigated everything carefully."[156] Luke also accompanied Paul on several of his missionary journeys, as evidenced by several "we" passages in the book of Acts.[157] Mark also wrote an NT book, and he received his information from Peter, who was an eyewitness.[158] Jude was not a direct eyewitness, but was closely associated with James, the brother of Jesus.

The Pseudepigrapha contains books written after Christ's death by authors who either wrote 'gospels' that were false or who pretended to be eyewitnesses when they weren't.

Readers should note that there are references in the Bible to other sources of information, such as the reference to the Book of Jashar in Numbers 21:14. This simply means other written works offer some helpful pieces of information, but they are not part of the Biblical canon. Similarly, I may refer you to a nutrition book to acquire information on sodium intake, but that resource is not the standard of ultimate truth.

If you're wondering after all of that *how* we can trust that we've gotten it right and have reached a consensus on the right book, ultimately faith must rely on God Whom has brought all things together for good to bring His true word to light. God, being a God of love, intends the best for His people, and His words are our life. This is why Deuteronomy 32:47 says, "For it is not an idle word for you; indeed it is your life. And by this word you will prolong your days in the land …" The Holy Spirit also convinces us in that the present Biblical canon finds validation in historical considerations and through the unified power the Word has on us when we read the Bible.

---

[154] II Corinthians 11:1-6, Galatians 1:8
[155] II Timothy 4:11
[156] Luke 1:1-4
[157] 16:10-17, 20:5-15, 21:1-18, 27:1-28
[158] I Peter 5:13

IV. Isn't the Bible self-contradictory?

This is a very important question. The short answer is 'no' because, as mentioned before, God is truthful, He is unable to lie, and He never contradicts Himself since all of His words are refined and tested.[159]

The great theologian Augustine once said, "If we are perplexed by any apparent contradiction in Scripture, it is not allowable to say, The author of this book is mistaken; but either the manuscript is faulty, or the translation wrong, or you have not understood."[160]

God never says anything hastily without thought nor is He divergent from His reliable character.[161] In addition, because God is omniscient, His thoughts are much higher than ours are,[162] and there are many secret things that God knows that we do not.[163] The apostle Peter tells us that some parts of the Bible are indeed "hard to understand."[164]

Finally, the truth is often difficult to digest, and we either reject that truth outright as non-truth[165] or recognize the truth as such but suppress it.[166] Our human perception is limited further by our inability to see the infinite, which Paul describes as looking into a dim mirror.[167] The Bible is a book written on many different levels, and one often finds that the deeper you go, ideas and concepts that originally were in opposition become revealed for what they truly are, eliminating the apparent contradiction. I don't want to casually breeze over this question, so I will expand much more on this in the next section.

Many people assume the Bible is farfetched from the start until something proves it right. The general problem with this

---

[159] II Samuel 7:28, Hebrews 6:18
[160] Augustine, "Reply to Faustus the Manichaean" in *A Select Library of the Nicene and Anti-Nicene Fathers of the Christian Church* (Grand Rapids: Eerdmans, 1956).
[161] Psalm 12:6, Proverbs 30:5-6
[162] Isaiah 55:9
[163] Deuteronomy 29:29
[164] II Peter 3:15-16
[165] Romans 1:18-19
[166] Romans 1:18-19
[167] I Corinthians 13:9

approach is that is makes life unlivable. In a Biblical sense, many shun what is superficially implausible, say, "That can't happen," and use that as 'proof' that the Bible is false. The problem with this approach is that all other fields reject it. When I see a patient who has a problem but I can't figure out what the diagnosis is, that doesn't mean the person's faking it (most of the time) or that his problem doesn't exist. It simply means I haven't asked enough of the right questions or dug deep enough to find an answer. If scientists gave up every time they encountered something they didn't 'get,' we would all be stuck in the Stone Age. A Bible student, then, follows the same blueprint as an astute scientist—that the unknown is not a contradiction or utterly unexplainable but a worthwhile endeavor that rewards those who faithfully seek, study, learn, analyze, and research.

V. How do I interpret the Bible?

A seminary professor of mine said that hermeneutics (Biblical interpretation) is about life, and your life invariably affects the way you interpret the Bible. No matter who you are your life experiences consciously and subconsciously affect what a verse means to you. Second, there is a distinct difference between *exegesis* and *eisegesis*. The former involves extracting meaning *from* the text; the latter involves putting your own meaning *into* the text. Whenever interpreting the Bible, always exegete and never, ever eisegete—otherwise, *you* are telling God what *you* think of *His* words. There is always a human temptation to reject what we read because we don't like what God has to say, which equates to a suppression of the truth.[168] The true meaning of the Bible never changes, but our perception of that meaning does.

The way to approach Biblical interpretation is to realize that it is the inspired Word of God and thus needs to be read literally, but in this literal interpretation, there can be *figurative*, *descriptive*, and *prescriptive* passages. The whole must always interpret the part, so one verse or a part of one verse should

---

[168] Romans 1:18

never be interpreted out of the context in which it was said. As the saying goes, "A text out of context is pretext." In other words, when reading anything, always ask yourself what was said before it, what was said after it, and what is the meaning of the text in the context of the entire Bible. *Context determines meaning* and *the whole interprets the part.*

For example, in Matthew 18:9 Christ says, "If your eye causes you to stumble, pluck it out and throw it from you. It is better for you to enter life with one eye, than to have two eyes and be cast into the fiery hell." Reading this passage literally yields some frightening conclusions, but in the context of Matthew 18, we see that Jesus is talking about several obstacles one ought to remove in walking a path of obedience. Hence, this is a figurative expression among other figurative expressions. Moreover, we can confirm this is figurative because Levitical law prohibits self-mutilation,[169] and Christ said Himself in Matthew 5:17 that He did not come to abolish the law but to fulfill it.

I've always liked how Mark Driscoll explains principles versus methods. He says, "Be careful not to confuse principles and methods. The principles of Scripture are timeless whereas the methods for obeying them are timely. The Bible allows both a closed hand of timeless truth and an open hand of timely methods. However, great error ensues when the two are confused. For example, Colossians 2:16 commands God's people to '[sing] psalms and hymns and spiritual songs.' This is the timeless Biblical principle. To be obedient we must then develop cultural methods by deciding when the church gathers, who leads the singing, what songs are chosen, how many times each song is sung, what instruments (if any) are used, etc."[170]

Latter revelations also supplant prior revelations. This view of progressive revelation applies because God did not reveal everything He had to say at once, and people's conditions change over time. For example, the Book of Leviticus is filled with prescriptions on what people should do if they sin, and this

---

[169] Leviticus 19:28
[170] Mark Driscoll, *On the New Testament* (Wheaton: Crossway, 2008), 42.

typically involves a form of animal sacrifice. However, Christ died and paid the ultimate atoning price for all sin for everyone,[171] so these animal sacrifices are no longer needed. Hence, Christ's atonement supersedes the prior revelation.

It is also imperative to understand that although the Bible is the Word of God, He worked through human authors to produce the text, and as a result, each author produced unique flavors of the Bible. This includes authors quoting other humans (for example, poets [172]), and using sad and mournful language (Lamentations). In many books, the author's personality seeps through. Luke, for example, who wrote the third gospel and Acts, was a physician, so he uses very technical Greek and is detail oriented. As a healer, he also writes from the perspective of curing those with (spiritual) ailments. The book of Isaiah is prophetic but is also very poetic.

It is everyone's responsibility to be disciplined,[173] to read and study the Word,[174] allow the Word *to guide him or her*,[175] memorize the Word,[176] obey the Word,[177] and seek, teach, and share the Word with others.[178]

VI. What's with so many Bible versions?

The best way to read either testament is in the original language, meaning Hebrew for the OT and Greek for the NT. However, this goal may be undesirable for many Bible students, so there are many English versions for you to choose from to assist you.

Literal translations seek to be as faithful to the original language as possible and translate word-for-word without any deviation. In seeking technical accuracy, some poetic or

---

[171] Hebrews 10:11-14
[172] Acts 17:28
[173] I Timothy 4:7
[174] Luke 2:46-52
[175] Psalm 119:105.
[176] Proverbs 22:17-19
[177] Hebrews 4:15
[178] Luke 19:10, John 4.

linguistic nuances are lost. These versions include the King James Version (KJV) and the New King James Version (NKJV), the New American Standard Bible (NASB), and the English Standard Version (ESV).

Functional equivalence translations take a broader approach, attempt to convey the main idea of a passage, and are not as particular about single words. Here, words may be added or deleted to express an idea or theme the original language conveys. The most popular version of this type is the New International Version (NIV) and the New Living Translation (NLT).

The New Revised Standard Version (NRSV) tries to be as literal as possible but also may be free some of the time to make an idea as accurate in English as it was in the original language. The NRSV also incorporates language that is more gender-neutral and uses peripheral information to expand on how it translates the text.

Paraphrased versions emphasize the broad theme of a narrative; as a result, specific words become less important in pursuit of the poetic essence of a passage. Examples include The Living Bible (TLB) and The Message (TM).

A concordance is a book that allows you to look up an English word and find the appropriate Greek or Hebrew word and its definition. A concordance is an invaluable tool for any student of the Bible because it allows you to obtain the true meaning of the text. A concordance won't teach you these languages, but knowing what particular words mean will help you to dig deeper into the text. The gold standard in concordances is *Strong's Concordance*. Many electronic Bibles offer an integrated concordance that allows you to click on any word and view a pop-up of the associated Hebrew/Greek words with definitions and descriptions.

VII. An Overview of the Books of the Bible

Old Testament

The OT starts with the words "In the beginning" and ends with the prophet Malachi about 400 years before the birth of Jesus. The OT details the start, development, and continuance of a relationship between God and His people. It moves through history, people, places, and events, but its main concern is how all these things relate to the divine purposes of God.

The main character of the OT is God, and all of the OT points toward Christ. For example, Moses was a mediator who liberated Israel from bondage, as Christ is the mediator between humanity and the Father. Jesus liberated us from sin and death. Isaac carried his own wood in preparation to be sacrificed by his father Abraham as Christ carried His own wooden cross and laid down his life for all of us. The blood of an innocent Passover lamb in Egypt spared the lives of Israel from God's judgment just as Christ's sinless and atoning blood produced the perfect sacrifice to save us all from condemnation. Jonah spent three days 'down below' in the belly of a great fish to eventually 'come up' and 'save' the city of Nineveh. Jesus rose from the dead three days later to save the whole world.

The *Pentateuch* (Genesis, Exodus, Leviticus, Numbers, and Deuteronomy) is the Bible's first five books and is also known as the Torah in Judaism. Pentateuch means "five-volume book" or "one book in five parts." Moses wrote the Pentateuch.[179]

Genesis is the Bible's first book and, thus, the book of beginnings. It explains how our world and universe began, and how humans, sin, and the plan for redemption began. Genesis details many relationships, such as those between God and the world, God and humankind, and humans and one another. Genesis introduces us to the 'founding fathers' of Christianity and highlights God developing a relationship with *individuals and families*, starting with Abraham and ending with Joseph. Here is where you'll also find the accounts of Adam, Eve, the Garden of Eden, Noah, and the flood. This book sets the tone for the rest of the Bible.

---

[179] Deuteronomy 31:24-26

Exodus marks the beginning of a relationship between God and a *nation* (Israel) as its people are liberated from oppression in Egypt through a mediator (Moses). This book lays a theological foundation as God reveals His name (Yahweh), His law, and how He is to be worshipped. The tabernacle, or the mobile sanctuary Israel used in the wilderness, is the single subject to which the Bible devotes the most time. Here, God reveals Who exactly He is so His people can engage in a covenant with Him.

The key theme of Leviticus is holiness. By now God has established a covenant with His people, and He gives them rules and guidelines on how to be holy by distinguishing themselves from the world. Laws on communal operation, sacrifices, and the priesthood are given. (In fact, there are more than 600 laws in the Pentateuch).

In Numbers, Israel moves from Mount Sinai to the border of the Promised Land, but because of murmuring, the Israelites are punished for their sin and forced to wander in the wilderness for 40 years. Disobedience prevented inheritance, but God remained faithful to the covenant He had with His people in spite of their sin.

In Deuteronomy, Israel is outside of the Promised Land and Moses passes away before entering. He transfers leadership to Joshua. Here, the law is repeated to the people to garner total commitment to and dependence on God to receive a blessing. At the end of his life, Moses uses this book to teach people how to live properly.

History Books (Joshua through Esther)

Joshua leads the people of Israel into the Promised Land through military conquest. The people cross over the Jordan River and the walls of Jericho fall by God's power.

In Judges, Israel is in the Promised Land but there is no central leadership. Generally, the people are apostate and do whatever they see fit. Yet in a time of crisis, God raises up judges who push back foreign oppressors and restore peace to the people.

Ruth, the main character of the eighth book, is a Moabite woman and the great-grandmother of King David. Ruth is selflessly devoted to Naomi, another widow. In a reflection of God's unceasing love, Boaz marries Ruth, and their offspring fall in the line that bears Jesus.

In I and II Samuel, we see the rise of kingship in Israel, starting with a man-chosen king who fails (Saul) followed by a God-chosen king who succeeds in some areas. David establishes a theocracy and rules from Jerusalem. In his rise from being an unknown to a national hero, David defeats Goliath.

I and II Kings: After King David dies, his son Solomon rises to power and becomes wealthy and wise beyond comparison. Solomon, however, falls into sin, and after he dies, the united Israel is divided into a northern kingdom (Israel) and a southern kingdom (Judah). The prophets Elijah and Elisha are introduced, and the book ends when the Babylonians lay siege to Jerusalem and the temple. The Israelites are exiled.

I and II Chronicles are an account of recorded history (especially of kings) to show Israel how badly they behaved, to show them God's covenants still exist, and to encourage obedience.

In Ezra, the exiles return home and begin to rebuild the temple in Jerusalem.

In Nehemiah, the exiles reconstruct Jerusalem's walls.

Esther, the main character in this book, acts as a mediator between the Persian king and the Jewish people to spare their lives and preserve the ancestors that would ultimately produce Jesus.

Wisdom and Poetry (Job to Song of Solomon)

Job tackles the issue of theodicy and exemplifies the great faith of the main character.

Psalms is the Bible's longest book and has over 100 hymns, laments, and songs of praise, remembrance, and thanksgiving.

Proverbs gives practical advice on how to live everyday life and live it wisely.

Ecclesiastes addresses the meaning of life and explains how to enjoy life. The true meaning of joy and work are also discussed.

Song of Solomon contains poetic love songs written by a man to his bride. This is the Bible's raciest book by far.

The Prophets (Isaiah to Malachi)

The NT quotes Isaiah about 400 times. Generally, Isaiah examines the dreadful effects of sin and disobedience, and then discusses the ultimate redemption of servants of God. Isaiah repeatedly looks ahead toward Christ.

Jeremiah is the 'weeping prophet.' He recurrently speaks about the punishing effects of sin, prophesizes against other nations, and details a new covenant with God's people in light of their failure to keep the law.

Lamentations is a melancholy book that examines sin and grieves about its destructive power.

Ezekiel is a prophet who spoke to the people from Babylon while in exile. He identifies sin as the cause of Babylonian captivity. He anticipates the return of the people to Judah and their restoration.

Daniel, who also prophesizes in Babylon, is a dream interpreter who is thrown into the lion's den and survives. He sees visions that allude to Christ in the future.

Hosea marries a prostitute, typifying God's faithfulness to His people who continually violate the covenant they have made with Him.

Joel looks forward to a day when history ends and the penalty for sin is paid. He also speaks of a plague of locusts that afflicts the people because of sin.

Amos attempts to call the people to repentance when their faith and obedience waver during a time of economic prosperity.

Obadiah condemns Edom for waging war against the people of God.

Jonah is called to preach to the evil city of Nineveh. The prophet tries to flee from God but becomes shipwrecked before being swallowed by a great fish and spending three days in its belly. Subsequently, the Ninevites see the error of their ways and are saved.

Micah speaks out against the people in a time of great inequality, when the 'haves' make their fortunes at the expense of the 'have-nots.'

Nahum proclaims judgment against Nineveh for harming God's people.

Habakkuk has faith but the people don't, and he speaks to God looking for clarity throughout this book.

Zephaniah confirms that the ultimate penalty for sin is death, yet God remains faithful to the promise to redeem those who believe in Him.

In Haggai, orders to rebuild the temple are given in preparation for Jesus's arrival.

Zechariah looks forward to Christ, attempts to call the apostate to repentance, and has visions meant to encourage the rebuilding of the temple.

Malachi is the last book of the OT and states that John the Baptist will come to pave the way for Christ.

New Testament

The NT is about everything that happened just before Christ was born, the life of Jesus, the experiences of his disciples, and the events in the early church. The main theme of the NT is the gospel or the good news that Christ has arrived and opened the door for everyone who believes in Him to be saved and have eternal life. Again, the main character of the NT is God.

The Synoptic (or "seeing together") Gospels are four accounts of the life and ministry of Jesus. Each gospel is characterized by the unique vantage point of the observer.

Matthew was a disciple, Jew, and tax collector. He writes to convince fellow Jews that Jesus is the Messiah. Hence, Matthew frequently relies on OT quotations.

Mark was not a disciple but a companion to the disciple Peter. His gospel is the shortest and speaks primarily to a Roman audience. He focuses on Jesus's actions and miracles.

Luke, a gentile, was not a disciple and heavily researched his book from eyewitness accounts. He was a doctor and, therefore, was very precise and detail oriented. He wrote to a gentile audience.

John was a disciple and a Jew. His gospel addresses the Greek-speaking world and goes into great detail about the person of Jesus. While the other three gospels are roughly similar, John stands apart as unique and personal.

Luke also wrote Acts. This book details the happenings of the early church, the spread of the gospel after Christ's ascension, Pentecost, and the conversion of Paul. Here, the Holy Spirit does many wonderful and marvelous things in the lives of believers.

The Epistles (or letters) were written to an individual or a church in a particular city. Each epistle was written with a purpose, and that purpose included to instruct others, correct incorrect doctrine, warn someone, or as a means of praise. Paul wrote most of the NT letters.

Romans is an extremely intellectual and theological letter written to those in Rome. Its aim is to explain the basic gospel and salvation, righteousness, and justification by faith. Essentially, Paul wrote to a church that hadn't received the gospel to describe what exactly the gospel is.

I and II Corinthians are two letters to the church in Corinth that was behaving badly and engaging in immoral behavior. Paul explains what appropriate Christian conduct should be, clarifies any confusion they had about their immoral behavior, and describes what proper interpersonal relationships should look like in the church.

Galatians can be summarized as *by faith alone through grace alone*. Here Paul corrects the fallacy that what we do actually saves us. Galatians says we are justified only by faith in Jesus, through the power of grace. The fruits of the Spirit are detailed here.

Ephesians is not a response to anything, but attempts to give readers a better understanding of the timeless purposes of God.

With this understanding and the high standard God has for the church, Paul describes how to fulfill that calling and be the best servant of Christ you can be.

Philippians was written to the church in Philippi to thank it for the monetary gift it sent to Paul. He encourages the church members to stand tall in times of crisis, promotes unity, and warns against those in their midst who wish to spread false doctrine.

Colossians refutes the heresies in the church at Colossae. Many secular ideologies mingled with Christianity, and Paul draws the line between what is true doctrine and what is false doctrine.

I and II Thessalonians was written to the young church in Thessalonica. Paul encourages new converts, inspires those facing persecution, and gives advice on how to live day-to-day. He corrects the false perception that Christ would be coming very, very soon.

I and II Timothy form the first part of the 'Pastoral Epistles.' Paul writes to Timothy who has been left to deal with the confusion that ensues after a church is established and needs some direction and guidance to steer the organization toward health. Church leadership is discussed.

Titus is a letter written by Paul to the man of the same name. He gives Titus guidance on opposition, warns against heresies, and details general instructions on proper conduct.

In Philemon, Paul writes a letter to this person on behalf of Onesimus. He encourages both men to demonstrate Christ-centered love for one another and conduct themselves in a manner befitting of Christians.

Hebrews demonstrates how Jesus is the ultimate fulfillment of the OT in every single way.

I, II and III John answers the question "How do I know I'm a Christian?" by explaining the life-altering changes being a Christian brings. These three books also debunk heresies.

I and II Peter serve as letters of encouragement and sources of strength for Christians enduring persecution for their faith.

The message of James is simple: faith produces works. In other words, when you call yourself a Christian, you will behave in a way that mirrors your new identity.

Jude is a warning against immoral people, false doctrines, and the power of such dangers to taint the pure doctrine.

Revelation is the Bible's final book, written by the apostle John to encourage believers and warn them to stay away from false or perverse forms of worship. Here at the end of the Bible is the goal of worship, just as the end of our Christian walk ends in the ceaseless, ordered, bountiful worship of God.

For Further Study

Craig A. Parton, *Religion On Trial* (Eugene, OR: Wipf & Stock, 2008).

Henrietta C. Mears, *What the Bible is All About* (Ventura, CA: Regal, 2007).

J. Scott Duvall and John Daniel Hays, *Grasping God's Word* (Grand Rapids, MI: Zondervan, 1995).

Norman L. Geisler and Thomas Howe, *The Big Book of Bible Difficulties* (Grand Rapids, MI: Baker, 1992).

Walter Bruggemann, *The Bible Makes Sense Revised Edition* (Cincinnati: St. Anthony Messenger Press, 2003).

Zondervan NASB Study Bible, ed. Kenneth Barker et al. (Grand Rapids: Zondervan Publishing House, 1995).

CHAPTER IV
CREATION & SIN

The doctrine of creation is important to understand, because it not only sets the tone for everything else to follow, but it also gives all believers profound insight into our very existence. If you are starting a business, you begin with a primary aim that guides all of your business activities. If you're building a tree house, you start with the thought of what you want to build in your mind, and your successful material execution follows that intangible blueprint. Every step that you take is structured and ordered from a single origin, a concrete focal point from which everything else flows. Creation is that concrete focal point of the human experience.

The doctrine of creation answers our most important questions: *Who* made us, *why* do we exist, *how* did we come into being, and *for what purpose*—in other words, this doctrine deals with the whole meaning of life. Certainly, a life that is unexamined will lead to frustration, confusion, and discontent. A life that is examined will lead to wisdom, knowledge, and understanding—and a life that is examined with the original blueprint from the Creator will lead to peace, happiness, joy, and fulfillment.

What Christians should know is that the doctrine of creation says God made the entire universe out of nothing. It says that He made it in order to glorify Himself, and that He made everything very good.

The creation narrative is located in the beginning of the book of Genesis, the Bible's first book. In Genesis, there are two major calls from God: (1) He calls the world into being. (2) He calls a special people to faithfully be His. As I will explain, the calls involve a gift given to creation, the stipulations that lay within the gift, and the divergent responses to that gift. The question then becomes *how* we will respond—with recalcitrant self-assertion or faithful obedience. The former response tends to dominate the narrative, leading to adverse consequences. The calls are rooted in a basic premise of the Bible that everything that follows is built upon: God and His creation are inextricably linked in unique and fragile ways.

Creation is a story about beginnings, and the story should be treated as a totality. So, when Genesis speaks about an individual, they should be regarded as representative of all creation, the part for the whole.[180]

I. In the Beginning

The Bible starts in Genesis 1:1 by saying, "In the beginning God created the heavens and the earth."

The first thing we should notice is that "In the beginning" is a phrase in Hebrew that denotes an indefinite period of time. (And speaking of time, we know that God is eternal and time*less*.[181] This means that when our universe was created, *our time* also began, which is why, for example, in each of the days of creation, there was a morning and an evening—both temporal events). In that beginning, Who was there? God was. He was present at the start, before our universe existed, because He *created*. The Bible begins with God, just as everything that we think, say, do, or believe ought to begin with God.

The heavens (plural) and the earth (singular) refers to the entire universe: our planet, celestial bodies, space, the stars, distant galaxies, and everything else that exists "out there." *Heavens* also implies the heaven where God dwells, angels, the invisible spiritual realm, and other heavenly beings.[182]

"In the beginning God created" also tells us that when God did create our universe, He made it out of nothing. The Hebrew

---

[180] Walter Brueggemann, *Genesis: Interpretation: A Bible Commentary for Teaching and Preaching* (Louisville: John Knox Press, 2010), 11.
[181] Deuteronomy 33:27; Psalm 90:2; Isaiah 57:15; I Timothy 1:17
[182] Nehemiah 9:6; Psalm 103:21, 148:2-5; Acts 4:24; Revelation 10:6

word for *created* is *bara*, which means to shape, fashion or create something from nothing. This is why throughout the Scriptures this word is only used with God as a subject. The Latin phrase *ex nihilo* is a fancy way of saying "out of nothing," which indicates that when God made the universe, nothing else existed but Him. In John 1:3 the Bible says, "All things came into being through Him, and apart from Him nothing came into being that has come into being."

Psalm 33:6 & 9 say, "By the word of the LORD the heavens were made, and by the breath of His mouth all their host ... For He spoke, and it was done; He commanded, and it stood fast."

Colossians 1:16 says, "For by Him all things were created, both in the heavens and on earth, visible and invisible, whether thrones or dominions or rulers or authorities—all things have been created through Him and for Him."

Why did God make anything? We are given insight into His motivation in Revelation 4:11: "Worthy are You, our Lord and our God, to receive glory and honor and power; for You created all things, and *because of Your will* they existed, and were created" (italics mine). In essence, all of creation is intended to reveal the glory of God. God made people specifically for His glory,[183] and the Psalms tell us that the inanimate creation is telling of God's glory as well.[184] The creation demonstrates the limitless power of God, His authority, His wisdom, and above all else, that what He has done well exceeds what could ever be conceived of or executed by any part of the creation.[185] The creation essentially reveals to us how great God is—yet He did not have to do any of it, because God does not need creation. In spite of this, He still gave all of us the free gift to enjoy.

And if anyone has ever wondered why people have an innate sense of creativity, the desire to do "big things" or the yearning to make things that are beautiful, then all you ought to do is consider Who made you. And, both at the end of each day of

---

[183] Isaiah 43:7
[184] Psalm 19:1-2
[185] Jeremiah 10:12, 14-16

creation and at the end of His six-day creative work, God saw all He had made and that it was good.[186] Yes, sin now exists in the world, but that does not negate the goodness of creation. This realization frees us all from a false sense of asceticism that seeks to reject the material world. Hence, in I Timothy 4:4-5, Paul says, "For everything created by God is good, and nothing is to be rejected if it is received with gratitude; for it is sanctified by means of the word of God and prayer." The point is that creation can be used in sinful, perverse, selfish, and destructive ways, but that does not mean the creation itself is inherently bad. Rather, it is *how we use* creation—either in a God-centered or a self-centered way. More on this a bit later.

A key point to be derived from the above verses is that the entire universe exists *because* of God, was created *by Him*, and was therefore *dependent on Him* to come into being. Without Him, there would be no us. And from a logical standpoint, this has to be the case because if anything existed before God or alongside Him, this would contradict the Biblical assertion that God is sovereign and rules over all. Accordingly, *nothing within or from* creation should ever be worshipped, because it is subordinate to God. Further, the denial that God made the universe *ex nihilo* means that something else is also eternal just like God. The implication, then, is that God is not sovereign, independent, or the only One worthy to be worshipped. And, since God made everything, we can be confident that *all* things come together for God's good purposes.[187] To deny that God made everything means that some things "just happened," are subject to chance, and are not part of His divine plan. The purpose of creation is already decided.[188]

Because creation is dependent, God is distinct from it. This does not mean, however, that God made everything and then went on break. God is *immanent*, or in other words, He remains in creation. As it says in Job 12:10, "In whose hand is the life of

---

[186] Genesis 1:4, 10, 12, 18, 21, 25, 31
[187] Romans 8:28
[188] Ephesians 1:9-10

every living thing, and the breath of all mankind?" Several other verses affirm the immanence of God.[189]

In Chapter II, I discussed Who God is and all of His attributes. We therefore know that God is wholly good, so anything that He makes will be good. God didn't begin creating out of malice or evil, because that would contradict His character. He began creating out of love—hence, in His infinite wisdom, God made you and me for something. To deny that reality means you accept as fact that your existence is pure happenstance and therefore devoid of meaning. Because if you weren't made for something, then all of reality is an exercise in futility that happened because of nothing and is doomed to become nothing. Therefore love, morality, trust, kindness, motivation, hope, faith, and family have absolutely zero meaning because they came from nobody and will all equate to nothing upon death. To deny that God exists, and that He has a positive intent for the world, is the most depressing, dehumanizing, wicked, malicious, and destructive ideology ever invented—because the way things are now is the best they will ever get, and the apex of existence rests on the shoulders of the inherent iniquity of humankind.

After God created the heavens and the earth in Genesis 1:1, the Bible says in verse 2 that "the earth was formless and void, and darkness was over the surface of the deep, and the Spirit of God was moving over the surface of the waters." (The reference to Spirit denotes Trinitarian activity). Formless and void is a phrase that means an uninhabitable wilderness. So, from what was uninhabitable and devoid of life, God will now proceed to make what is inhabitable and vibrant.

Genesis 1:3-26 consists of the account of the six days of creation. At the start of each day, God speaks something into existence. For example on the third day, verses 9-13 says, "Then God said, 'Let the waters below the heavens be gathered into one place, and let the dry land appear'; and it was so. God called the dry land earth, and the gathering of the waters He called seas; and God saw that it was good. Then God said, 'Let the earth sprout vegetation, plants yielding seed, *and* fruit trees on the earth bearing fruit after their kind with seed in them'; and it was

---

[189] Acts 17:25, 28; Colossians 1:17; Ephesians 4:6; Hebrews 1:3

so. The earth brought forth vegetation, plants yielding seed after their kind, and trees bearing fruit with seed in them, after their kind; and God saw that it was good. There was evening and there was morning, a third day."

On the first day, God separated the light and darkness, thereby making day and night; on the second day, God created an expanse that separated the heaven above it and the waters below it; on the third day, God made dry land, the seas and plant life; on the fourth day, God made the sun, moon, and all the stars in the sky; on the fifth day, God made sea animals and birds; and on the sixth day, God made the land animals and also formed Adam and Eve.

On each day we notice several recurring themes: (1) The entire process is *structured and ordered*, so there is no randomness that generates order. Therefore, not only is there intelligent design, but the Designer is well beyond our comprehension. Each day has an assigned task, and only certain things are made in each day. (2) There is *distinction and separation*. Different things are different, so God clearly distinguishes them. Light is separated from darkness, and the heavens are separated from the waters. (3) Each day has a beginning and an end signified by the fact that there was "evening and morning." In other words, within each segment of creation, there was a clear start and stop time. God stopped creating a particular thing when the day was over and did not go back to create more. (4) God *spoke* everything into existence with the exception of humans. (5) What God made was already mature and fully developed. And when God spoke, things happened *immediately*. He didn't make baby stars that would grow up to be big stars—He made them fully formed. The same is true of living creatures—birds, cattle, and creeping things were created fully formed. He didn't make prototypes of things that would evolve or "improve" into better versions. To suggest anything else means that God made what wasn't good, and therefore had to get better. This ties in to the final point: (6) Everything that God made was good. Because God is good, He is only capable of making what is good, and thus He didn't make anything that was subpar, inferior, or questionable. Also, within the goodness of creation is a unity, and that unity is ethical as well as aesthetic.[190]

II. The Bible versus Science

If one reads Genesis 1 and a science textbook, it would seem that the two narratives are incompatible. Genesis tells us that God made the world in six literal 24-hour days, and that everything happened quickly. Evolutionary science tells us that the Earth is billions of years old and things happened very, very slowly. In the end, what should not divide Christians on creation is *how* as long as we agree on *Who*. The Who is irrevocably God, and the Bible is a theological statement on why God made our world and us. Theologically, for example, do interpretations other than six literal days in Genesis 1 change the fact that Christ died and atoned for our sins? No. Does this change the Trinity? No. Does this change the fact that we are saved by faith alone through grace alone? No.

Quite simply, that is an argument to have in the basement of the church, but never in the main sanctuary.

III. The Story of all of Us

The creation of human beings was very special. The first reason for this is that God gave humans a purpose. In the first five days of creation, the text just says God said, and it happened. On the sixth day, God gave us more thought. Genesis 1:26 says, "Then God said, "Let Us make man in Our image, according to Our likeness; and let them rule over the fish of the sea and over the birds of the sky and over the cattle and over all the earth, and over every creeping thing that creeps on the earth." (The Us and Our are also Trinitarian references). Image and likeness refer to something that is similar but not the same. Hence, all of us are a *representation* or an image of God and *like* God, but we are not God. Our imperfect image reflects the perfect example of God.

---

[190] Genesis 1:31

The fancy way of referring to humans being made in the image of God in Latin is *Imago Dei*.

As representations, then, human beings have many attributes like God, such as morals; a conscience that gives us an inner sense of right and wrong; an invisible, intangible spirit; an intellect and the ability to reason; a complex ability to express ourselves and communicate that animals lack; the capacity for love, truth, justice, holiness; and finally, a relational nature. The relational nature of humankind as a function of being made in God's image thus brings us into relationship with God, other humans, the rest of creation and ourselves.

Second, humans are special because no other part of creation carries this distinction of being God's image bearers. And, because of this distinction, humans have *dominion* (from the word *rada* meaning to rule or subjugate) over the rest of creation. However, dominion *does not* mean exploitation. It *does* mean to secure the well being of other parts of creation. In a Biblical sense, leadership always equals servitude.[191]

Verses 27-31 says, "God created man in His own image, in the image of God He created him; male and female He created them. God blessed them; and God said to them, 'Be fruitful and multiply, and fill the earth, and subdue it; and rule over the fish of the sea and over the birds of the sky and over every living thing that moves on the earth.' Then God said, 'Behold, I have given you every plant yielding seed that is on the surface of all the earth, and every tree which has fruit yielding seed; it shall be food for you; and to every beast of the earth and to every bird of the sky and to every thing that moves on the earth which has life, I have given every green plant for food'; and it was so. God saw all that He had made, and behold, it was very good. And there was evening and there was morning, the sixth day."

Third, note *how* God made us in Genesis 2:7a: "Then the LORD God formed man of dust from the ground." (From this point onward, I will use man and woman as figurative representations of all men and all women. Adam and Eve are our distant

---

[191] John 10:11

parents, and generally speaking, represent the male and female sides of humanity).

The word *formed* derives from the Hebrew word *yasar*, which means to mold or shape in a more intimate sense—as a potter molds clay. Figuratively then, God had "a hand" in making Adam. God *spoke* everything else into existence but took the time to *form* us, and then He *breathed* life into us. We are more like Him than any other part of creation. Genesis 2:7b says, "[The LORD] ... breathed into his nostrils the breath of life; and man became a living being." The Bible does not say that God breathed the breath of life into any other part of creation. Furthermore, God speaks directly *only* to humans[192] and addresses them individually as "you."[193] This demonstrates God's commitment to us.

Woman was created in Genesis 2:18. The text says, "Then the LORD GOD said, 'It is not good for the man to be alone; I will make him a helper suitable for him.'"

As I mentioned before, God was already in a Trinitarian relationship before He made human beings, so of course it makes sense that we, made in the image of God, ought to be in a relationship as well. Thus, Adam needed a helper *because he needed help* and he, being alone and not in a relationship, was a bad idea. The text says that in the created order during the time before Eve was made, the physical world, including the beasts of the field, were unsuitable to help Adam. So, God "caused a deep sleep to fall upon the man, and he slept; then He took one of his ribs and closed the flesh at that place. God fashioned into woman the rib which He had taken from the man, and brought her to the man."[194] Note as well that God did not make another man for Adam to be with—He fashioned a woman. If, then, man ought not to be alone, the solution to that solitude is *not* another man.

These few verses are packed with information that many in modern society become confused with. Here are a few key points:

---

[192] Genesis 1:28
[193] Genesis 1:29
[194] Genesis 2:21-22

(1) Adam and Eve are made from the "same stuff." If I were to choose a word in Greek to express that idea it would be *homoousia*. God did not make Eve independently from Adam because she was never meant to be separate from Him. She literally was made from Adam's rib and therefore the two of them are equals, yet "man does not originate from woman, but woman from man; for indeed man was not created for the woman's sake, but woman for the man's sake" (I Corinthians 11:8-9).

(2) Yet within their equality, there is deference. Adam was made first, and Adam was given the privilege of "naming rights." Genesis 1:19 says that God brought "every beast of the field and every bird of the sky, and brought them to the man to see what he would call them." Did God need Adam to name anything? No, but God gave Adam the free gift and privilege of doing so as a *steward* of God's creation. Adam was the creator of nothing, but he had been *given privilege* over creation *only* because of God. Adam was given the right to name Woman, or Eve (Genesis 2:23), as well. Notably, Adam's stewardship was meant to be enjoyed as God demonstrated, but *stewardship can never be confused with ownership*. Being a proper steward means taking responsibility for and tending to what ultimately is someone else's. This means (all men please listen very carefully), that God has given us a free gift, and yes, that gift comes with privileges. But we should never, ever act as if we "own" anything, because we don't. Everything we were, are, and ever will amount to be is *because of God*, not us. Which means when we look at ourselves, we say, "I am a child God." So act like it. When we look at women, we say, "They are all children of God." So treat them as such. When we look at creation, we say, "The LORD made this for us." So treat it as such. And when we look at God, we say, "Thank you LORD, for You are Almighty, and I am your humble servant. Without You, I am nothing, and everything I do is to glorify the One Who made me." Act as if you believe this truth.

(3) Adam and Eve's identity is a function of mutual dependence. Eve was made *because* Adam needed help and Adam needed help *because* he would fail by himself. Man and Woman separately *serve different functions*, and considering the male and female forms naked is a fitting example of this. The male and female bodies by themselves are non-productive and are incapable of producing life, as are two of the same forms. In order to generate life and to fulfill God's first command to creation ("Be fruitful and multiply"[195]), they absolutely need each other.

(4) *Deference does not mean inequality.* Of course, in modern society, no one wants to be labeled "the help." But "helping" stems from the Trinitarian formulation of love, and from that love, deference. For example, the Holy Spirit is called a "Helper" throughout the New Testament,[196] and without the Holy Spirit, we would be incapable of living Christ-centered lives. Is there anything "subordinate" or unworthy about the Holy Spirit?

In fact, in John's gospel, the word Helper comes from the Greek *parakletos* that also means an intercessor, consoler, advocate, comforter, or *someone called to one's side*. Jesus is referred to as a Helper and the primary *parakletos* by implication in John 14:16. And in I John 2:1, we are told Jesus is the *parakletos* that advocates for us to the Father. Therefore, if Jesus didn't "help," no one will be able to advocate for us and atone for our sins. Even further, to illustrate deference as a Trinitarian concept, all one has to do is examine the passage from Philippians 2:3-9, "Do nothing from selfishness or empty conceit, but with humility of mind regard one another as more important than yourselves; do not merely look out for your own personal interests, but also for the interests of others. Have this attitude in yourselves which was also in *Christ Jesus, who, although He existed in the form of God, did not regard equality with God a thing*

---

[195] Genesis 1:28
[196] John 14:16, 15:26, 16:7

to be grasped, but emptied Himself, taking the form of a bond-servant, and being made in the likeness of men. Being found in appearance as a man, He humbled Himself by becoming obedient to the point of death, even death on a cross. For this reason also, God highly exalted Him, and bestowed on Him the name which is above every name" (italics mine).

In other words, Jesus is the ultimate example of equality with deference, because even though He is fully God, He emptied Himself and, for our sake, took the form of a human being. His obedience led to His death, and that obedience brought Him exaltation.

If I were to briefly sum up Genesis 1 and 2, I would say it describes God's calling of the world into existence. From that calling, we are able to define (1) our origins, (2) our identity, and (3) our purpose. We can only know what we are meant to do if we know who we are. That identity, in turn, is based exclusively on the One from Whom we came. An identity fuels a purpose, and a purpose based on a false identity leads to failure. God made you, so why would you look anywhere else to find your life's mission statement? It naturally follows, then, that any misunderstanding about our purpose or who we are is rooted in an incorrect formulation of Who we came from, leading to confusion, anxiety about what to do with ourselves, and a life filled with identity crises. A firm acknowledgement in the divine craftsmanship of God fulfills us all and allows us to embrace our true identity.

IV. An aside to discuss oneism

This section talks about alternative models for creation and why they fail. It is designed to make you aware of modern heresies and provide you with a defense against false doctrine. If you would like to continue reading about creation and sin, please skip ahead to section V.

Many people would suggest that to embrace faith means to reject reason and, therefore, to deny what can be perceived with the senses. This idea is based on a philosophy of "oneism"—that everything in our known universe fits within the confines of a box. Here, the universe began inside the box without external influences, and everything that *is*, *was*, or *will be* must be defined *within* the confines of that box. All phenomena, therefore, need not have a cause or a purpose—rather, all that is needed is an explanatory mechanism (how) based upon the rules established within the closed system (also, one need not consider *why* the box is there or *who* established the rules of the box). And since there is no reality outside of the box, the pinnacle of existence occurs during our lifetime. There was nothing before, and thus, there is nothing after. Oneism suggests that reality (the whole box) came out of nothing and is ultimately fated to become nothing. Atheism and theism thus have a common trait at a single point: out of nothing came something. A divergence exists in what happens before and after that point.

In "twoism," there is something outside of the box, and that other thing can communicate with, speak to, and interact with our box. In twoism, another entity exists in the universe separate and distinct from our human world. In this paradigm, God certainly does exist and can move between the two boxes. Here, our reality is a function of another reality, and that other reality will follow rules and norms foreign to us. Further, that other reality *must* be superior to ours because in order to create, design, and influence another box, the first box must have more power, knowledge, skill, and talent, just as a painter creates an image that resembles, *but is subordinate to*, himself.

In oneism, Christ is not God but a regular human being just like you and me. Of course, He existed, but He couldn't possibly be God, because He comes from the same system as you and me—at best, He can be a great role model or teacher. Men, women, grass, plants, animals, and different religions, for example, are all the same because we all come from the exact same raw material. No one element has dominion over another, there is no separation among groups, and thus, a rock is equal to a young boy.

Now, allow me to take a moment to explain the problem of bias. Pretty much everyone has the same amount of information, knowledge, and resources in front of them—we all have access to the Bible, we all have access to scientific information about the known universe, and we all live in a time where information (in most of the world) is freely disseminated. Yet despite having the same data, some people are staunch atheists, and others are devout believers in God. Why? Bias. In our thinking, we all have certain predispositions toward ideology, and our upbringing, experiences, and environment will mold how we perceive the world. This cardinal bias ultimately forms each of our belief systems. Like it or not, we all are guilty in some form of this prejudice, and Haynes described this phenomenon to be the boggle line.

A "famous" atheist once said that he could not *prove* God does not exist in much the same way that he could not prove the tooth fairy does not exist, but based upon the sheer mathematical improbability of God's existence, atheism, for him, was a foregone conclusion. True, I also cannot prove God doesn't exist, nor can I prove that God *does* exist. Where does that leave me but in a nebulous void where I must subjectively choose which path to follow based upon preference?

Ironically, a cornerstone of belief in God is predicated on the fact that nonbelief *has to be* a very real possibility. Belief and hoping in the unseen, or faith, *actually requires the possibility that the subscriber be wrong*. For if that possibility did not exist, there would be no conscious trust on the part of the believer—if not, what you're left with is coercion. After all, if I splash you with a bucket of water and then tell you that water is wet, there's absolutely no room for argument. Keep in mind that God never forces your hand. He *invites* you to freely and graciously commit.

In oneism, why have hope if the best we can do is right here on Earth? Why excel in life if, once you die, you cease to exist? Why dream unless those wishes can materialize here and now since their effectiveness is nullified upon death? Why ever care for another or practice self*less*ness instead of choosing to maximize one's own potential at the expense of others?

One depressing defeat for oneism lies in the reality that it inevitably leads to nonexistence, which paints a picture of humanity even more tainted than the one that already exists. There will be no ultimate justice, no ultimate mercy, no redemption, no salvation, and no future. To subscribe to oneism means to deny God's existence and to pretend that all the treacherous, cruel behavior in this world will never face judgment from the divine Judge, and all immorality and licentiousness is valid and acceptable behavior to an indifferent, void universe that regards all of humanity as happenstance. Oneism means you accept every perverse, wicked, cruel, malicious, and destructive desire man has ever produced and embrace such debauchery with the casual indifference that accepts that this is the way things will be. Oneism permanently condones the suffering of the innocent and celebrates in the triumph of evil. Oneism applauds the pride that fuels its own convictions; it directs all honor and glory toward the self in the perpetual festival of self-interest.

Another depressing defeat for oneism is the absence of primary causality. Everything in our world has a cause and also has its resultant effect. If a tree falls down in the forest, it's because a lumberjack decided to get some wood. If a car explodes, it's because someone threw a match into the gas tank. If there's an earthquake, it's because tectonic plates shifted. If everything in our world has a known, established cause, and science strives to seek out and explain such causes, why would any rational mind accept that the original starting point of our world is that it "just happened" *without* a definite cause? In fact, the ultimate fallacy of oneism lies at its genesis: how can a causeless, purposeless megaphenomenon (the big bang) spawn a universe that follows rules antithetical to itself?

We live in a world so blinded by its own desire for all to be the same that we have begun sacrificing the truth for mixtures and derivations of the truth so that all may feel welcome with their own perception of reality. The truth, in and of itself, is mutually *exclusive*. If the truth were mutually *inclusive*, then it would not be the truth but an accommodation. Earth functions in the manner we're all used to because gravity remains constant at 9.8 m/s². If this number were 13.4 or 7.4, the world as we know it would cease to exist. The truth does not waver, yet people tend to waver between two opinions, hopping from branch to branch.

Ultimately, we are each faced with the one cardinal question in life: shall we choose to believe that *we* are the pinnacle of all existence, or is there something else greater than us that does, in fact, exist? Statistics and reason tell us that *both scenarios are equally improbable. T*o what conclusion, then, will reason lead us? It could be to neither and that we are simply asking the wrong question, yet common sense suggests that all answers will essentially boil down to more-than-oneism or oneism. For each, every person's boggle line segregates the acceptable from the implausible, but implausibility is a matter of perspective. What you believe, therefore, has little to do with the actual facts but *how those facts are perceived by you*. And this perception is built upon the security of certainty—reason finds comfort in the tangible, observable, and familiar, while faith challenges you to take a risk and venture into the unknown. Furthermore, at some point, the certainty itself can be idolized, dissolving the importance of whatever the certainty *is in*. (Also consider that life as we know it *is not,* in fact, certain but based on assumptions about reality and significant likelihoods).

In my experience, I have come to the conclusion that faith does not negate reason, but the former is the ultimate expression of the latter. (In fact, as the former Pope John Paul II suggests in his thirteenth encyclical, *Fides et Ratio*, faith less reason leads to superstition and reason less faith leads to nihilism). Hence, the intersection of faith and reason is the point where reason finally admits its own deficiencies and submits to the higher authority. If oneism were true, randomness still *could not* create an ultimate form of reason in an ultimate form of life because, as with any other observable system, anything that is influenced by chance *will tend to regress to a mean*. This means that based on oneism, human beings are mediocre compromises who, in their mediocrity, have formulated (at best) an ordinary, yet wholly inadequate, explanation for their own origins. This realization begs, then, to ask a very striking question: if mediocrity, in the pursuit of certainty, can produce a very unlikely yet theoretically plausible answer, what would superiority, unhindered by the rules of oneism, produce with total assurance?

The cardinal danger of oneism, then, points to one inescapable and horrid reality: idolatry. Since God does not exist, something has to take His place, and that something is therein exalted as supreme.

V. The Fall & Sin

The history of humanity is saturated with individuals born into sin who revolt against God, thereby separating themselves from Him. In the end, everyone knows that sin is bad. When you commit a sin, you have a good idea that what you did was wrong, but what is sin, where did it come from, and why is it so bad?

Wayne Grudem defines sin as "any failure to conform to the moral law of God in act, attitude, or nature." [197] The great theologian Augustine said that pride is the root of all sin in that it directs all attention toward the self and away from God. If we were all made for *His* glory, sin directs our efforts away from God, rejecting our purpose and our Creator. Sin is lawlessness,[198] unrighteousness,[199] that which is a violation of the laws given by God,[200] or the unwritten laws written on our hearts.[201] Sin is also the failure to what is right when you know what is right.[202]

---

[197] Wayne Grudem, *Systematic Theology: An Introduction to Biblical Doctrine* (Grand Rapids: Zondervan, 1994), 490.
[198] I John 3:4
[199] I John 5:17
[200] Romans 2:17-29
[201] Romans 2:15
[202] James 4:17

So ... back to creation. We know by now that everything that God made was "good" and therefore God neither created sin nor is He to be blamed for sin because He is perfect and just.[203] The reason sin is bad is very simple: the wages for sin is death.[204] So if God didn't create sin, what did happen?

In Genesis 3:1-7, we find out: "Now the serpent was more crafty than any beast of the field which the LORD God had made. And he said to the woman, 'Indeed, has God said, "You shall not eat from any tree of the garden"?' The woman said to the serpent, 'From the fruit of the trees of the garden we may eat; but from the fruit of the tree which is in the middle of the garden, God has said, "You shall not eat from it or touch it, or you will die."' The serpent said to the woman, 'You surely will not die! For God knows that in the day you eat from it your eyes will be opened, and you will be like God, knowing good and evil.' When the woman saw that the tree was good for food, and that it was a delight to the eyes, and that the tree was desirable to make one wise, she took from its fruit and ate; and she gave also to her husband with her, and he ate. Then the eyes of both of them were opened, and they knew that they were naked; and they sewed fig leaves together and made themselves loin coverings." Sin had now entered into creation.

Up until this point in Genesis, God gave only one negative command: "From the tree of the knowledge of good and evil you shall not eat, for in the day that you eat from it you will surely die" (Gen 2:17).

The serpent in the Garden of Eden asked one of the most loaded questions in the entire Bible. Essentially, the snake said, "Did God *really* say?" Had Eve been totally focused on God, there is only one appropriate response: walk away in recognition that something is questioning God.

This is what God said in Genesis 2:16-17, "From any tree of the garden you may eat freely; but from the tree of the

---

[203] Deuteronomy 32:4
[204] Romans 6:23

knowledge of good and evil you shall not eat, for in the day that you eat from it you will surely die."

This is what Eve *said that God said* in Genesis 3:2-3, "From the fruit of the trees of the garden we may eat; but from the fruit of the tree which is in the middle of the garden, God has said, 'You shall not eat from it *or touch it*, or you will die.'"

The mistake that Eve made was that she gave the serpent an audience, gave it time to speak, and then *entertained* what the serpent said. (In fact, it's very important to note that the snake tempted Eve simply by talking to her). Subsequently, the serpent made a direct assault on three of God's truthful, honest, and good promises that *He had already provided*: (1) the truth that Adam and Eve would die if they ate; (2) the command to do what is lawful and not eat from the tree of the knowledge of good and evil; and (3) their identity as subordinate creations and not an omnipotent Creator. Another way of saying this is that the serpent appealed to the carnal nature inside of Eve by appealing to the (a) lust of the flesh, (b) the lust of the eyes, and the (c) pride of life. All of these types of sins are mentioned in I John 4:16. This is why Eve, "saw that the tree was good for food,[a] and that it was a delight to the eyes,[b] and that the tree was desirable to make one wise.[c]" Still another way to say it is that Eve was (a) tempted by a biological need, (b) saw something worthwhile that would make her "better," and (c) could make her better than just a "mere woman"—"empowered," "independent," and just like God. What the snake didn't tell Eve is that all of these false goals carry a hefty price.

Another way to analyze the interaction between the serpent and Eve is to go back to Genesis 2:15-17. There, human creatures are given a *vocation* ("cultivate and keep"), *permission* ("From any tree of the garden you may eat freely") and a *prohibition* ("from the tree of the knowledge of good and evil you shall not eat).[205] The divine assignments should be considered as a whole, and each task obtains validation in the context of the other two.

---

[205] Walter Brueggemann, *Genesis: Interpretation: A Bible Commentary for Teaching and Preaching* (Louisville: John Knox Press, 2010), 46.

The serpent persuaded Eve to focus on the *prohibition* so that she forgot what God had already given. As a result, the prohibition does not remain a safeguard but a limitation and a barrier to individual growth and autonomy. In other words, the serpent made God's protection look like a threat and God's commands were now *optional*.

Although the serpent tempted Eve, Adam still ate. Had Adam led and not followed, this never would of happened. Had Eve obeyed and not succumbed, none of this would have happened. Blaming "the man" or blaming "the woman" is a pointless exercise and directs attention from the real problem: the selfishness that lurks inside all of us and the pride that rejects God.

The cataclysmic effect of the Fall of Man is that the sin of Adam (not the sin of Eve) was imputed to all of humanity, and thus all of humanity was counted guilty. This is summed up nicely by the apostle Paul in Romans 5:12-21, "Therefore, just as through one man sin entered into the world, and death through sin, and so death spread to all men, because all sinned ... death reigned from Adam until Moses, even over those who had not sinned in the likeness of the offense of Adam, who is a type of Him who was to come ... For as through the one man's disobedience the many were made sinners." Essentially, God made creation and it was good, but Adam's sin tarnished that creation, and Adam, having sinned and therefore becoming a sinner, could not have offspring that were sinless because what is corrupted cannot make what is incorruptible—sin is that powerful and pervasive. Adam's sin gave us a sinful nature,[206] our whole being became corrupt,[207] and apart from Jesus, we are incapable of doing good or pleasing God.[208] The bottom line is that because "there is no man without sin"[209] all people are guilty before God and no one is righteous.[210]

---

[206] Psalm 51:1-5, 58:3; Ephesians 2:3
[207] Jeremiah 17:9; Romans 7:18; Ephesians 4:18; Titus 1:15
[208] Isaiah 64:6; John 8:34, 15:5; Romans 8:8; Ephesians 2:1-2; Hebrews 11:6
[209] I Kings 8:46
[210] Romans 3:9-18

The penalty for sin is death, so whether it's Sin with a big "S" or sin with a tiny "s" the penalty remains the same. So one ought not get technical and try to put sin in a hierarchy by studying instances where Jesus refers to *greater* sin [211] or lesser commandments[212] or The LORD refers to an abomination.[213] Sin equals death. Period.

Sin not only destroys you, but separates you from God.[214] Even thinking about sin brings sin to life, and such thoughts lead to death.[215] Sin leads to internal conflict and strife,[216] has deleterious environmental consequences,[217] leads to more sin[218] and enslaves you to it.[219] Sin grieves the Holy Spirit[220] and is characterized by immorality, thievery, greed, idolatry, drunkenness,[221] lying, and cowardice.[222] Sin also results in events of mass destruction;[223] envy, slander, malice, deceit, and hypocrisy;[224] destruction of interpersonal relationships;[225] physical illnesses;[226] hatred, confusion, desire, impatience, viciousness, faithlessness, harshness, and impulsivity.[227] (Please keep in mind that sin *can* cause all of the above things but that does not mean sin *always* causes these things. For example, Christ was sin*less* but experienced some of the most horrific and barbaric things ever known).

To go back to the concept of helper for a moment, please pay special attention to who God called after Eve ate the fruit. Eve is

---

[211] John 19:11
[212] Matthew 5:19
[213] Leviticus 18:22
[214] Isaiah 59:2
[215] James 1:15
[216] I Peter 2:11
[217] Leviticus 18:24-25
[218] Romans 6:19
[219] John 8:34; Romans 6:16
[220] Ephesians 4:30
[221] I Corinthians 6:9-11
[222] Revelation 21:8
[223] Jude 1:7
[224] I Peter 2:1-5
[225] Genesis 3:12-13
[226] John 5:8, 14
[227] Galatians 5:19-21

the *helper*, which means she is *not* the one who is ultimately accountable. This is why even though Adam and Eve both sinned, God called on Adam only: "Then the LORD God called to the man, and said to him, 'Where are you?'" (Genesis 3:9). With privilege comes responsibility.

To highlight just how quickly sin disrupts what is good, pay attention to how many times Adam uses the term "I" after God calls him. Genesis 3:10-13 says, "'*I* heard the sound of You in the garden, and *I* was afraid because *I* was naked; so *I* hid myself.' And [God] said, 'Who told you that you were naked? Have you eaten from the tree of which I commanded you not to eat?' The man said, 'The woman whom You gave to be with me, she gave me from the tree, and *I* ate.' Then the LORD God said to the woman, 'What is this you have done?' And the woman said, 'The serpent deceived me, and I ate'" (italics mine).

Before sin, Adam sang (Genesis 2:23) about how great Eve was. Eden was filled with mutuality and equity. After the fall, Adam can't stop blaming Eve for what happened. Impartiality turned into control and distortion. Since sin disrupts relationships, Adam separated himself from Eve and labeled her as "defective" and something that a "defective God" gave him. Adam has now become the center of his own universe, so if he fails, it can't be his fault. God, women, circumstances, weight, race, drugs, class, upbringing, friends, habits, politics, height, eye color, and ideology all become crutches upon which man falls in order to dismiss himself of all responsibility. Any man that abuses his God-ordained position to take authority must always first consider that when God comes knocking at your door, it doesn't matter who did what. He holds you accountable *first*.

Yet, the story doesn't end there, because sin does not overpower God, and Jesus will ultimately conquer sin. That is, while sin (and therefore death) reigned because of one man, the sins of all of humanity were paid for by the death and atoning sacrifice of Jesus. One man condemning everyone is a bad deal. The best deal is everyone being set free by one man: Jesus.[228]

---

[228] Romans 5:12-21

Finally, it compels us all to think that the choices Adam and Eve made not only were foolish but irrational. They lived in the Garden of Eden, a place pure, pristine, and untainted where scarcity did not exist nor did pain, heartache, or suffering. But for the illusory chance to be like God, they both believed a lie that offered a false assurance of gain when, in actuality, Adam and Eve needed nothing. Through this voluntary act, Adam and Eve turned away from God and pursued a course of self-interest, and ironically, in the end they both got what they wanted: knowledge of good and evil. But neither considered the cataclysmic cost their choice would have. The serpent, representative of Satan,[229] is fully aware that he cannot overpower God, so he does the next best thing and lures God's creation away from Him. Lucifer was the first to rebel against God, and he persistently tries to lure us away from God as well.

Before I move on, it is worth mentioning that Genesis 3 is frequently treated as the origin of sin and evil in the world, but this assumption is false. We know this because Lucifer rebelled against God *prior* to our creation. The Bible, generally speaking, does not concern itself with how evil *came into the world* but rather *how we respond to it*. Walter Brueggemann says, "There is no hint that the serpent is the embodiment of principle of evil. The Old Testament characteristically is more existential. It is not concerned with origins but with faithful responses and effective coping. The Bible offers no theoretical statement about the origin of evil ... Similarly [the fall] is taken as an account of the *origin of death* in the world. That assumption is based upon the mechanistic connection of sin and death ... A variety of responses to the reality of death are offered, most often assuming that while certain forms of death may be punishment, death in and of itself belongs properly to the human life God wills for humankind."[230] God's main concern is always life. Our concern thus ought to be how we can answer God's call and *live* by His terms.

---

[229] Revelation 12:9
[230] Walter Brueggemann, *Genesis: Interpretation: A Bible Commentary for Teaching and Preaching* (Louisville: John Knox Press, 2010), 41-42.

VI. Conclusion

A helpful way to view the entire creation narrative is first to realize that God didn't have to do any of it, nor did He need creation. But because He is a relational, loving God, He claimed His ownership over creation by giving it all away as a free gift. (And as mentioned before, that gift comes with stipulations). He made us as the dominant stewards of that free gift. And because God is timeless, He already knew that when He made us, we would reject Him, but He went ahead anyway. Why? Because that's how powerful God's love is—He can say yes to us even when we say no to Him. And it's proper that creation was made on His terms, because we are the dinner guests, and He is the host.

His love becomes even more apparent in how He reacted after Adam and Eve sinned. God responded to those who rejected Him by providing for them: "The LORD God made garments of skin for Adam and his wife, and clothed them" (Genesis 3:21).

And when you think about this logically, Adam and Eve *had* to be kicked out of the Garden, because if not, they could have eaten from the tree of life (thereby sustaining their immortality) and for eternity be doomed in their fallen state. There would be no atonement, no salvation, and no release from sin. Still, even though the serpent intended to mock God and spit in His face through temptation and sin, *death now served a purpose.* The devil thought death would be his championship ring, but now the death of those who believed would be the ticket into heaven for eternity. And God, knowing humans would reject Him beforehand, also knew they could not come back to Him without His help. So, in his unceasing love, God pre-decided to save creation by sacrificing Himself for all of us. So *before* Adam and Eve were kicked out of the Garden of Eden, God already had a plan for deliverance. He tells the serpent, "Because you have done this, cursed are you more than all cattle, and more than every beast of the field; On your belly you will go, and dust you will eat all the days of your life; and I will put enmity between you and the woman, and between your seed and her seed; He shall bruise you on the head, and you shall bruise him on the heel" (Genesis 3:14-15). The 'He' who "shall bruise" points directly to Jesus.

The serpent thought he could outdo God, but God already had a plan. Adam and Eve thought they could be like God, but He already knew what would happen. All of their mishaps and failures would now set up the single greatest phenomenon in the entire history of known existence: the Incarnation, life, death, and resurrection of Jesus Christ. God simply refuses to leave the world alone.

It now becomes clear how *all* things work together for good for God's purposes.[231]

For Further Reading

Walter Brueggemann, *Genesis: Interpretation: A Bible Commentary for Teaching and Preaching* (Louisville: John Knox Press, 2010).

---

[231] Romans 8:28

CHAPTER V
THE INCARNATION, LIFE, DEATH, AND RESURRECTION OF JESUS CHRIST

This chapter of *What Christians Should Know* will complete the examination of the core or essential doctrines of the Christian faith. Certainly, Christianity is much, much more than five principles, but these central tenets lay the foundation upon which everything else is built. The remaining chapters will continue to educate on other basic doctrines, ideas, and principles.

All Christians must fully understand the gravity of Who Jesus Christ is to all of us. He, *and He alone*, is the only path to the Father, to salvation,[232] and to eternal life. This is why in John 14:6, Jesus says, "I am the way, and the truth, and the life; no one comes to the Father but through Me." The path to Heaven, the path of atonement, and the path to forgiveness of sins is irrefutably and exclusively through Jesus. There are not multiple ways, there is only one way.

Accordingly, to deny that Jesus is *the only way* is heresy. This is why Jesus says in Matthew 10:33, "But whoever denies Me before men, I will also deny him before My Father who is in heaven." Rejection of Jesus is a rejection of God,[233] and irrevocably leads to death. In what follows, I will explain why Jesus is so important and why Christless Christianity is formless and void.

---

[232] Salvation refers to the deliverance from sin and the consequences of sin.
[233] I John 2:23; II John 9

I. The Incarnation and Person of Jesus Christ

Essential Doctrine #2: What Christians should know is that Jesus Christ is fully God and fully man in one person.[234]

That is, Jesus is unchangeably, indivisibly, and inseparably a union of human and divine natures in one being, not parted or divided into two persons, with the property of each nature being preserved.[235]

A simple way of saying this is that Jesus, remaining what He was (God), became what He was not (a man), and will be so forever.

The Incarnation of Jesus really is the rescue mission that God executed in order to save humanity. The word *incarnate* means to embody in flesh or to take form. So God *became* a human being and took the form of a human being by becoming flesh.[236] And this becoming did not happen after Jesus was born so that a human became God. Instead, Jesus was conceived by the work of the Holy Spirit and His virgin mother, Mary. Jesus did not have a human father. Matthew 1:18-20 says:

> Now the birth of Jesus Christ was as follows: when His mother Mary had been betrothed to Joseph, before they came together she was found to be with child *by the Holy Spirit*. And Joseph her husband, being a righteous man and not wanting to disgrace her, planned to send her away secretly. But when he had considered this, behold, an angel of the Lord appeared to him in a dream, saying, "Joseph, son of David, do not be afraid to take Mary as your wife; for the Child who has been conceived in her is *of the Holy Spirit*" (italics mine).

In Luke's account of Christ's birth, His conception is explained in more detail.

---

[234] This is often referred to as a hypostatic union.
[235] From the Chalcedonian Creed, 451 A.D.
[236] John 1:14; Philippians 2:7

> Now in the sixth month the angel Gabriel was sent from God to a city in Galilee called Nazareth, to a virgin engaged to a man whose name was Joseph, of the descendants of David; and the virgin's name was Mary. And coming in, he said to her, "Greetings, favored one! The Lord *is* with you." But she was very perplexed at this statement, and kept pondering what kind of salutation this was. The angel said to her, "Do not be afraid, Mary; for you have found favor with God. And behold, you will conceive in your womb and bear a son, and you shall name Him Jesus. He will be great and will be called the Son of the Most High; and the Lord God will give Him the throne of His father David; and He will reign over the house of Jacob forever, and His kingdom will have no end." Mary said to the angel, "How can this be, since I am a virgin?" The angel answered and said to her, "The Holy Spirit will come upon you, and the power of the Most High will overshadow you; and for that reason the holy Child shall be called the Son of God."[237]

As a result, *the conception* of Jesus was very miraculous, but *His birth* was very ordinary.[238] The virgin birth affirms that Jesus is not some ordinary guy who has a mom and a dad just like you and me. Because He is fully God and fully man, He is very special, and His conception was necessarily miraculous. Because Mary never engaged in sexual intercourse to conceive Jesus, there was no effort on her part. This affirms that our salvation *has nothing to do with human works* and is totally and completely dependent on God. If Jesus did simply have a regular mom and dad that conceived Him, it certainly would be hard for anyone to believe that "god" was conceived in the same way you and I were. Furthermore, Jesus was born holy,[239] sinless,[240] and thus *without any of the legal guilt of sin or inherited moral corruption as a*

---

[237] Luke 1:26-35
[238] Luke 2:7
[239] Luke 1:35
[240] II Corinthians 5:21; I Peter 2:22; I John 3:5

result of Adam. Nowhere in the Bible does it say that sin is inherited from the father only, nor does it say that Mary was sinless. What the Bible does say in Luke 1:35 is that *through the power of the Holy Spirit* overshadowing the virgin Mary, the child she would give birth to would be holy. Christ also was without sin throughout His entire life,[241] and always conducted Himself in a manner pleasing to the Father.[242] Jesus is a "lamb unblemished and spotless."[243]

The birth of Jesus was not unexpected. His birth fulfilled several prophecies from the Old Testament, the same Scriptures that Judaism uses as its authoritative Word. The first allusion to Christ comes in Genesis 3:15, when God says that the seed *of the woman* (not the man) would crush the head of the serpent. Isaiah 7:14 says, "Therefore the Lord Himself will give you a sign: Behold, a virgin will be with child and bear a son, and she will call His name Immanuel." (Immanuel means "God is with us.") This prophecy is fulfilled in Matthew 1:18, 22-23. Micah 5:2 tells us where Jesus would be born, in Bethlehem: "But as for you, Bethlehem Ephrathah, too little to be among the clans of Judah, from you One will go forth for Me to be ruler in Israel. His goings forth are from long ago, from the days of eternity." Matthew 2:1 fulfills this prophecy. Finally, Malachi 3:1 tells us that Jesus will enter the temple in Jerusalem: "'Behold, I am going to send My messenger, and he will clear the way before Me. And the Lord, whom you seek, will suddenly come to His temple; and the messenger of the covenant, in whom you delight, behold, He is coming,' says the LORD of hosts." This prophecy is fulfilled in Matthew 21:12-13 and Mark 11:15. And because the temple in Jerusalem was destroyed in 70 A.D., we know that all of these events had to happen before that date, and they did.

The Incarnation highlights the intimacy God has with His creation. Jesus chose to enter into our physical realm as one of us in order to save us. This means that Jesus had breakfast, used the

---

[241] John 15:10
[242] John 8:29
[243] I Peter 1:19

bathroom, and sat down and had dinner with His family just as you and I do. And He did this because God does not leave creation alone. He became one of us so we can say we have a savior who is very personable and who experienced everything that we do, including temptation,[244] weariness,[245] hunger,[246] and thirst;[247] He also grew[248] and had to study in order to learn and become wise.[249] He learned how to become obedient,[250] had a soul, and experienced personal turmoil.[251] Jesus has a real, human, physical body.[252] He is not an impersonal God detached from our reality who rules from afar, and it is *because* Jesus "was tempted in that which He has suffered, He is able to come to the aid of those who are tempted."[253]

Furthermore, it's one thing to say that Jesus was just a human being. It's another thing to fully embrace the idea that Jesus had to be fully human in order to save humanity. The full humanity and full deity of Christ is beautifully articulated in the timeless classic, On the Incarnation by Athanasius.

Athanasius wrote *On the Incarnation* in defense of Christ's full divinity and *against* Arianism, an emerging theology of the time that suggested Christ was begotten from the Father, therefore not eternal, and thus subordinate to the Father.

Had Christ not been wholly divine, Athanasius argues, then Christ would have needed a mediator Himself to bring us into *koinonia* (fellowship or community) with God, and that imperfect mediator would therein need another mediator, creating an endless succession of imperfect mediators without any resultant salvation. In short, in order to re-create creation and turn the corruptible (humans) back into the incorruptible,

---

[244] Hebrews 4:15
[245] John 4:6
[246] Matthew 4:2
[247] John 19:28
[248] Luke 2:40
[249] Luke 2:52
[250] Hebrews 5:8
[251] Matthew 26:38; John 11:35, 12:27
[252] Luke 24:39, 42; John 20:17, 20, 27
[253] Hebrews 2:18

God needed the same substance, or Jesus, in order to bring that imperfect back to being perfect. Athanasius brilliantly argues that the entire process is motivated by the love of God for His creation, and to suggest that He would impart upon us a less than perfect mediator would in fact demote and diminish that love motivation to less than steadfast, permanent, perpetual, and all-encompassing.

Athanasius says, "It was our sorry case that caused the Word to come down, our transgression that called out His love for us, so that He made haste to help us and to appear among us. It is we who were the cause of His taking human form, and for our salvation that in His great love He was both born and manifested in a human body."[254] He also says, "The Word perceived that corruption could not be got rid of otherwise than though death; yet He Himself, as the Word, being immortal and the Father's Son, was such as could not die. For this reason, therefore, He assumed a body capable of death, in order that, through belonging to the Word Who is above all, and, itself, remaining incorruptible through His indwelling, might thereafter put and end to corruption for all others as well, by the grace of the resurrection."[255]

Further explanation as to why Jesus incarnated is best summarized in Hebrews, a book of the New Testament addressed primarily to Jewish converts familiar with Old Testament prophecy. The theme of Hebrews is the absolute supremacy and sufficiency of Jesus as the revealer and mediator of God's grace. In essence, Hebrews illustrates that the bridge between humanity and God is Jesus. In 2:14-17 it says:

> Therefore, since the children share in flesh and blood, [Jesus] Himself likewise also partook of the same, that through death He might render powerless him who had the power of death, that is, the devil, and might free those who through fear of death were subject to slavery all

---

[254] Saint Athanasius, *On the Incarnation: Enhanced Version* (Grand Rapids: Christian Classics Ethereal Library, 2009), 4, Kindle.
[255] Ibid, 9.

their lives. For assuredly He does not give help to angels, but He gives help to the descendant of Abraham. Therefore, He had to be made like His brethren in all things, so that He might become a merciful and faithful high priest in things pertaining to God, to make propitiation for the sins of the people.

Jesus is our great high priest, not only because He is God but because He was also fully a man. As a result, He knows exactly what it's like to live on earth, deal with everyday problems, and struggle with real issues. Hebrews 4:14-16 says:

> Therefore, since we have a great high priest who has passed through the heavens, Jesus the Son of God, let us hold fast our confession. For we do not have a high priest who cannot sympathize with our weaknesses, but One who has been tempted in all things as we are, yet without sin. Therefore let us draw near with confidence to the throne of grace, so that we may receive mercy and find grace to help in time of need.

Hebrews 2:17 uses the word *propitiation*. The term refers to turning away God's wrath (see Leviticus 16:20-22, 17:11). *Propitiation* comes from the word *hilaskomai* in Greek, meaning, "to atone for sin, to render one's self, to make reconciliation or to expiate." In other words, Christ could only represent us before the Father if Jesus became one with us. In order for Jesus to turn aside the wrath of God against guilty sinners, He had to become one with us and die as a substitute for us.

Why did Jesus *have to be* fully human?

To start, Adam was the first man, and his disobedience in the Garden of Eden condemned all of humanity.[256] Jesus is the last Adam[257] or the "second man"[258] so that "through one act of righteousness there resulted justification of life to all men. For as through the one man's disobedience the many were made

---

[256] Genesis 2:15-3:7
[257] I Corinthians 15:45
[258] I Corinthians 15:47

sinners, even so through the obedience of the One the many will be made righteous."[259] Since God cannot be mocked,[260] His original intent to have humankind rule over creation[261] is fulfilled through the perfect obedience of Jesus, who can thus rule over all creation.[262]

Second, because God is perfectly just, He is incapable of saying "never mind" to sin. So, while He is merciful and may want to forgive us, a penalty must be paid for the sin that we have committed. And that debt must be paid because, as we all know from the last lesson, the wages for sin is death.[263] Propitiation is thus necessary because sin is incompatible with God and is offensive to His character. He may forgive sins, but if a price is not paid, then God would be merciful, but not just, which is contrary to what the Bible teaches us. And, from a logical standpoint, a God that is merciful at the expense of being just is a pushover, and people are free to do what is right in their own eyes.

Third, one day we will all stand before God to face judgment.[264] If humanity is separated from God because of sin, only one person can serve as a mediator for us and bridge the gap between God and humans: a person who is both fully God and fully human. And this makes perfect, logical sense because how could God, being perfect, accept anything less than a perfect mediator to vouch for us? In order for God to save *human beings*, Jesus had to be a *human being*—if someone is owed $100, they will not accept apples for payment. Even more, because salvation comes only and exclusively *from God*,[265] nothing from creation (which is finite and corrupt) could save us. But the eternal and timeless Jesus could, Who *can* bear the full penalty of sin. This is why in I Timothy 2:5 it says, "For there is one God, and one mediator also between God and men, the man Christ Jesus."

---

[259] Romans 5:18-19
[260] Galatians 6:7
[261] Genesis 1:26-28
[262] Matthew 28:18; Luke 19:17; Ephesians 1:22; Hebrews 2:9; Revelation 3:21
[263] Romans 6:23
[264] Romans 14:12; II Corinthians 5:10
[265] Jonah 2:9

Fourth, the Bible is filled with imperfect people who all tried to be obedient and faithful but failed, so Who can we look to as a human example on how to be divine? Jesus. He is the blueprint that we must follow: "The one who says, 'I have come to know Him,' and does not keep His commandments, is a liar, and the truth is not in him; but whoever keeps His word, in him the love of God has truly been perfected. By this we know that we are in Him: the one who says he abides in Him ought himself to walk in the same manner as He walked."[266]

Fifth, when Jesus's physical body rose from the dead, it served as a model by which all of humanity can follow to inherit a new, imperishable body raised in glory.[267] This is why after the resurrection, Jesus appeared to many in a physical, tangible, and "flesh and bones" body.[268]

II. The Cross

> Then the soldiers of the governor took Jesus into the Praetorium and gathered the whole Roman cohort around Him. They stripped Him and put a scarlet robe on Him. And after twisting together a crown of thorns, they put it on His head, and a reed in His right hand; and they knelt down before Him and mocked Him, saying, "Hail, King of the Jews!" They spat on Him, and took the reed and began to beat Him on the head. After they had mocked Him, they took the scarlet robe off Him and put His own garments back on Him, and led Him away to crucify Him. As they were coming out, they found a man of Cyrene named Simon, whom they pressed into service to bear His cross. And when they came to a place called Golgotha, which means Place of a Skull, they gave Him wine to drink mixed with gall; and after tasting it, He was unwilling to drink. And when they had crucified Him, they divided up His garments among themselves by casting

---

[266] I John 2:4-6; cf. Romans 8:29; I Corinthians 3:18; I Peter 2:21
[267] I Corinthians 15:42-49; Colossians 1:18
[268] Luke 24:39-43; John 20:25-27

lots. And sitting down, they began to keep watch over Him there. And above His head they put up the charge against Him which read, "THIS IS JESUS THE KING OF THE JEWS." At that time two robbers were crucified with Him, one on the right and one on the left. And those passing by were hurling abuse at Him, wagging their heads and saying, "You who are going to destroy the temple and rebuild it in three days, save Yourself! If You are the Son of God, come down from the cross." In the same way the chief priests also, along with the scribes and elders, were mocking Him and saying, "He saved others; He cannot save Himself. He is the King of Israel; let Him now come down from the cross, and we will believe in Him. HE TRUSTS IN GOD; LET GOD RESCUE Him now, IF HE DELIGHTS IN HIM; for He said, 'I am the Son of God.'" The robbers who had been crucified with Him were also insulting Him with the same words. Now from the sixth hour darkness fell upon all the land until the ninth hour. About the ninth hour Jesus cried out with a loud voice, saying, "ELI, ELI, LAMA SABACHTHANI?" that is, "MY GOD, MY GOD, WHY HAVE YOU FORSAKEN ME?" And some of those who were standing there, when they heard it, began saying, "This man is calling for Elijah." Immediately one of them ran, and taking a sponge, he filled it with sour wine and put it on a reed, and gave Him a drink. But the rest of them said, "Let us see whether Elijah will come to save Him." And Jesus cried out again with a loud voice, and yielded up His spirit. (Matthew 27:27-50)

The crucifixion of Jesus Christ was one of the most heinous, barbaric events in the history of the world, yet this horrific event demonstrates the unceasing love of God for His creation. The crucifixion and death of Christ did not have to happen, but "God so loved the world, that He gave His only begotten Son."[269] The cross, then, simultaneously represents the love and justice of God

---

[269] John 3:16; cf. Romans 5:8

because Jesus dying on the cross *atoned* for our sins. Atonement in a general sense refers to the work done by Jesus in His life and death. Atonement in a specific sense refers to the debt of sin paid by Jesus through His death on the cross. The atoning blood sacrifice of Jesus was absolutely necessary because even if God's wrath is turned away, something still absolutely needs to pay the price of sin, because God is perfectly just.

Essential Doctrine #3: ***Penal substitutionary atonement*** **refers to the fact that Jesus bore the penalty of sin in His death, He was a substitute sacrifice for us all, and that penal substitution atoned for humanity, thereby reconciling us back to God.**

It must be recognized that before Christ's sacrifice atoned for our sins (and thus changed *our* relationship with God), the death of Christ had an effect on the relationship of God *with us*. Before Christ, there could be no redemption. With Christ, there is redemption for all of humanity.

The blood of Jesus therefore irrevocably pays the full debt owed because of sin. The precursor to this event in the Old Testament is the Day of Atonement, or modern-day Yom Kippur. In Leviticus 16 (long before Christ's death), once a year the high priest would make an atonement offering for the sins of the people of Israel. Two goats would be used—one to be sacrificed and the other as a scapegoat that would be sent out into the wilderness. The sacrificed goat would bear the penalty of the people's sins, and the scapegoat was sent out in order to remove the sin from the midst of the people.[270] Subsequently, God could pass over the sins of Israel. An earlier example in the Old Testament of the wrath of God "passing over" the people is first seen in Exodus 12 when the innocent blood of a Passover lamb protects the people of Israel as God "passes over" those houses marked with blood on the doorposts and lintel.

---

[270] Leviticus 16:10

The slaughtered goat acted as a *propitiating* sin offering. That is, the people had sin, and the goat acted as a substitute to pay the price for that sin. The sacrificed animal *temporarily* atoned for sin by replacement, and throughout the Old Testament, blood sacrifice is intimately linked to atonement.[271] After slaughtering the first goat, the high priest would lay hands on the second goat, confess the sins of the people and then send the scapegoat far out into the wilderness to die.[272] This symbolically represented *expiation* or the removal of the people's sins by taking them "away." The goat's going away or being "cut off" coincides with other instances where separation from God's people means punishment for sin.[273] Again, *propitiation* (the slaughtering of the goat) diverts God's wrath by blood sacrifice. But, while God's wrath is diverted because a debt has been paid, the people are still guilty and "dirty" because of their sin. Hence, *expiation* (the sending away of the scapegoat) achieves "cleanliness" and purity; it removes the guilt and shame of sin. Propitiation turns away God's wrath. Expiation removes sin and its effects. Both are integral parts of atonement or reparation for a wrong. The purpose of propitiation and expiation was to restore the relationship between God and His people, of course.

Note also that, in both cases (propitiation and expiation), the high priest serves as a mediator between God and the people. Back then, the high priest was an imperfect mediator capable only of temporizing measures. Jesus is the perfect mediator whose sacrifice is permanent and eternally sufficient.

The atonement of Jesus was simultaneously necessary for our sake, but *not* necessary for God's sake. God did not have to save humanity at all, but He did because of love. God, for example, did not save the angels who rebelled against Him,[274] and that action is perfectly just. Hence, as a result of God deciding to save humanity, the sacrificial atonement of Jesus

---

[271] Leviticus 17:11
[272] Leviticus 16:22
[273] Leviticus 7:20-27; 17:4, 8-14; 18:29; 19:8; 20:3, 5-6, 17-18
[274] II Peter 2:4

became necessary.[275] As a result, when Jesus died on the cross, He had already lived a life of active obedience fully and completely fulfilling the requirements of the law. Christ suffered for *our* sake and then died on the cross for *our* sake and died for *our* sin.[276] Yet it is important to remember that the *life* of Christ was characterized by the absence of sin *and* exemplary righteousness.

Therefore, the death of Christ is as important as the life of Christ, because in order to be reconciled to the Father, one needs more than lack of sin. One also needs to have an upstanding character to be in fellowship with God. God isn't neutral but overwhelmingly good, so in order to commune with Him, we have to strive higher. Such righteousness comes *only* from God: "And may be found in Him, not having a righteousness of my own derived from the Law, but that which is through faith in Christ, the righteousness which comes from God on the basis of faith."[277] If the *life* of Christ was not important, He could have passed away immediately after birth. But because He lived a righteous life without sin, He can serve perfectly as our representative to the Father. As it should be clear by now, everything that has to do with our salvation *happens as a function of God alone.*

Essential Doctrine #4: What Christians should know is that we are saved by grace alone and through faith in Jesus Christ alone.

> Nevertheless knowing that a man is not justified by the works of the Law but through faith in Christ Jesus, even we have believed in Christ Jesus, so that we may be justified by faith in Christ and not by the works of the Law; since by the works of the Law no flesh will be justified. But if, while seeking to be justified in Christ, we ourselves have also been found sinners, is Christ then a minister of

---

[275] Luke 24:25-26
[276] Isaiah 53:6, 12; John 1:29; II Corinthians 5:21; Galatians 3:13
[277] Philippians 3:9

> sin? May it never be! For if I rebuild what I have *once* destroyed, I prove myself to be a transgressor. For through the Law I died to the Law, so that I might live to God. I have been crucified with Christ; and it is no longer I who live, but Christ lives in me; and the life which I now live in the flesh I live by faith in the Son of God, who loved me and gave Himself up for me. I do not nullify the grace of God, for if righteousness comes through the Law, then Christ died needlessly.[278]

For the sake of simplicity, "works" and "law" refers to things that you do and rules that you follow. Both are incapable of saving anyone because if that was the case, Christ did not have to be crucified and die for our sins.

This is why religion saves no one, but Jesus saves everyone. This idea also nullifies any human effort, because if we are not saved by the free gift of God only, then that means that we, as sinful creations, can do something and win God over. This is false, heretical doctrine and essentially tells God "we can control you." This central fact is one of the key differentiation points of Christianity from every other religion on planet Earth. Isaiah says based on our own works, the best we can offer God are filthy rags: "For all of us have become like one who is unclean, and all our righteous deeds are like a filthy garment; and all of us wither like a leaf, and our iniquities, like the wind, take us away" (64:6).

> But now apart from the Law the righteousness of God has been manifested, being witnessed by the Law and the Prophets, even the righteousness of God through faith in Jesus Christ for all those who believe; for there is no distinction; for all have sinned and fall short of the glory of God, being justified as a gift by His grace through the redemption which is in Christ Jesus; whom God displayed publicly as a propitiation in His blood through faith. This was to demonstrate His righteousness, because in the

---

[278] Galatians 2:16-21

forbearance of God He passed over the sins previously committed; for the demonstration, I say, of His righteousness at the present time, so that He would be just and the justifier of the one who has faith in Jesus.[279]

And, through that propitiation we regain God's favor (because we are sinners) *not* by anything that we do but *by the gift of His grace only, through faith in Christ only.*

Propitiation is also discussed in I John 4:10, "In this is love, not that we loved God, but that He loved us and sent His Son to be the propitiation for our sins."

Isaiah 53:5 says, "But He was pierced through for our transgressions, He was crushed for our iniquities; The chastening for our well-being fell upon Him, And by His scourging we are healed."

I Corinthians 15:3 says, "For I delivered to you as of first importance what I also received, that Christ died for our sins according to the Scriptures."

I Peter 3:18 says, "For Christ also died for sins once for all, the just for the unjust, so that He might bring us to God, having been put to death in the flesh, but made alive in the spirit."

I John 2:2 says, "And He Himself is the propitiation for our sins; and not for ours only, but also for those of the whole world."

Hebrews 2:17 says, "Therefore, He had to be made like His brethren in all things, so that He might become a merciful and faithful high priest in things pertaining to God, to make propitiation for the sins of the people."

Now that the context and meaning of the crucifixion is clear, we shall proceed to the event itself.

The crucifixion was a barbaric, brutal and arduous ordeal. The event was so catastrophic that the word excruciating was invented to describe it. When Mark 15:24 simply says that, "they crucified Him," it does not fully convey the pain of the whole ordeal. In fact, crucifixion was the ultimate form of punishment

---

[279] Romans 3:21-26

in the Roman empire, typically reserved only for those individuals guilty of crimes against the state. Crucifixion was banned against Romans, and Jesus was crucified in the center[280] of the other two men executed that day. The center spot was reserved for the most despicable of "scum" according to the Romans.

Before the crucifixion, Jesus was flogged by Romans soldiers. As Dr. Alexander Metherell states in *The Case for Christ*:

> Roman floggings were known to be terribly brutal. They usually consisted of thirty-nine lashes but frequently were a lot more than that, depending on the mood of the soldier applying the blows.
>
> The soldier would use a whip of braided leather thongs with metal balls woven into them. When the whip would strike the flesh, these balls would cause deep bruises or contusions, which would break open with further blows. And the whip had pieces of sharp bone as well, which would cut the flesh severely.
>
> The back would be so shredded that part of the spine was sometimes exposed by the deep, deep cuts. The whipping would have gone all the way from the shoulders down to the back, the buttocks, and the back of the legs. It was just terrible.[281]

In fact, taking the flogging and crucifixion in total, the event was so terrible that Jesus was tortured beyond recognition, as prophesized by Isaiah.[282]

Dr. Metherell mentioned that some people die from the flogging alone, but Jesus's suffering was far from over. In fact, all the bleeding from the flogging caused so much blood loss that Jesus presumably had low blood volume and therefore was weak, dizzy, and thirsty as He carried His own cross to be crucified. This may explain why Jesus collapsed en route to Golgotha.

---

[280] John 19:18
[281] Lee Strobel, *The Case for Christ* (Grand Rapids: Zondervan, 1998), 195.
[282] Isaiah 52:14

Although Christ was sinless, He suffered tremendously on the cross, and crucifixion essentially meant a slow death by suffocation. Although the barbaric procedure normally took hours, in come cases, the afflicted would wait for days before they passed away. Basically, the criminal's arms were outstretched and fastened by nails on a wooden cross. The five to seven inch nails went through *the bones* of the wrist (not the palm), and therefore crushed a major nerve in order to secure the body onto the cross. Routinely, the wrists were nailed very far away from the body, and so both of Jesus's shoulders would have been dislocated to anchor Him into place. Jesus therefore would have had to support His entire bodyweight with His arms because His feet were nailed into the cross as well. Since His chest was stretched upward and sideways, it became very difficult to exhale against severe pressure. The only option for exhalation was for Him to pick up His body by the strength of His arms, tugging at the skin and soft tissue nailed into the hard, splintered wood. His torture was agonizing, and just to take a breath, He had to add to His agony. Thus crucifixion was an experiment in anguish where the simple act of breathing became a prolonged, unbearable experience.

And keep in mind that Jesus did all of this as a free loving gift even while being spat upon, mocked, and ridiculed. So if anyone ever asks you, "What has God done for you?" you can confidently affirm the living hell our Lord and Savior endured for humanity.

In addition to the physical pain, Jesus also suffered the psychological pain of being scoffed at while helpless. In fact, before the crucifixion, in the Garden of Gethsemane, Jesus sweated blood,[283] a rare yet medically possible phenomenon (hematidrosis) that only occurs under times of severe stress. And Jesus also had to suffer the emotional trauma of bearing the burden of sin for all of humanity. He, being holy, found sin detestable but had to bear the burden of all of our guilt despite His utter revulsion toward evil. Jesus was also alone on the cross,

---

[283] Luke 22:44

having been abandoned by His disciples[284] and had no means of consolation. This is why Jesus cried out, "Eli, Eli, lama sabachthani?" that is, "My God, My God, why have You forsaken Me?"[285] because bearing the burden of sin separated Him from fellowship with God, Who unleashed His full fury and wrath toward sin against His only Son.

Hundreds of years before Christ was crucified, Isaiah predicted that the debt owed to God would be paid,[286] and when Jesus recognized that He had paid the full penalty for sin, He said, "It is finished."[287] This one-time, sufficient[288] payment in full frees us all from condemnation.[289] Jesus shed His blood on the cross, and His precious blood was the ransom paid to free us from sinful ways,[290] cleansing our conscience,[291] removing the barriers between ourselves and God,[292] *progressively* cleansing us from sin,[293] and conquering death and the accuser.[294]

The removal of barriers is illustrated in Matthew 27:51, which says, "And behold, the veil of the temple was torn in two from top to bottom; and the earth shook and the rocks were split." In the temple in Jerusalem, the veil separated the most holy place from the rest of the temple. In essence, in a building that symbolically represented barriers and precise stipulations that distanced God and man now had the divider between where God is and where we are torn.

Without Christ, we all deserve death and God's wrath because of sin. That sin subsequently separates us from God, and enslaves us to sin. Christ sacrificed Himself to pay the penalty of sin,[295] to propitiate for us,[296] to bring us back into relationship

---

[284] Matthew 26:56
[285] Matthew 27:46
[286] Isaiah 53:11
[287] John 19:30
[288] Hebrews 9:25-28
[289] Romans 8:1
[290] I Peter 1:18-19
[291] Hebrews 9:14
[292] Hebrews 10:19
[293] I John 1:7; Revelation 1:5
[294] Revelation 12:10-11
[295] Hebrews 9:26

with God,[297] and to redeem us out of sin.[298] Yet propitiation, expiation, and atonement alone will bring us back to "zero" having turned away God's wrath and having paid the price for sin. God even takes it a step further and *justifies* us.

II Corinthians 5:21 says, "He made Him who knew no sin to be sin on our behalf, so that we might become the righteousness of God in Him."

Justification is a legal construct from the Greek word *dikaioo*. God considers all of our sins immediately and instantaneously forgiven *and* He also declares us righteous as a function of Christ's righteousness. God predestined everyone He would call, and "these whom He called, He also justified; and these whom He justified, He also glorified." [299] The entire process is God-dependant and human-exclusive. Justification comes as a function of faith in Jesus only[300] and no one can condemn those who God has elected.[301] God imputes the righteousness of Christ into us.[302] So Adam's sin was imputed to all humankind, all that sin is then imputed to Jesus, and the righteousness of Jesus is imputed to all who have faith and believe in Him.

In Galatians 2:6, Paul elaborates and says, "Nevertheless knowing that a man is *not justified by the works of the Law but through faith in Christ Jesus*, even we have believed in Christ Jesus, so that we may be justified by faith in Christ and not by the works of the Law; since by the works of the Law no flesh will be justified" (italics mine).

Without justification, we would *not* be righteous in the eyes of God and thus unable to live eternally with Him.

---

[296] I John 4:10
[297] II Corinthians 5:18-19
[298] Mark 10:45; Hebrews 2:15; Titus 2:14
[299] Romans 8:30
[300] Romans 5:1
[301] Romans 8:33-34
[302] Romans 4:3, 5:17; I Corinthians 1:30

III. The Resurrection

Essential Doctrine #5: What Christians should know is that Jesus was crucified and died on the cross, and on the third day, He rose from the dead.

> But on the first day of the week, at early dawn, they came to the tomb bringing the spices which they had prepared. And they found the stone rolled away from the tomb, but when they entered, they did not find the body of the Lord Jesus. While they were perplexed about this, behold, two men suddenly stood near them in dazzling clothing; and as the women were terrified and bowed their faces to the ground, the men said to them, "Why do you seek the living One among the dead? He is not here, but He has risen" ... And behold, two of them were going that very day to a village named Emmaus, which was about seven miles from Jerusalem. And they were talking with each other about all these things which had taken place. While they were talking and discussing, Jesus Himself approached and began traveling with them. But their eyes were prevented from recognizing Him. And He said to them, "What are these words that you are exchanging with one another as you are walking?"[303]

The resurrection of Christ fulfills Old Testament prophecies that occurred 700 years before the event itself.[304] Christ also prophesized about His own death and that He would rise three days later.[305]

Effectively, the entire New Testament is a collection of books written by people who were either eyewitnesses to the risen Christ, or who obtained their information from people who were direct eyewitnesses. The apostle Paul, who had a direct and personal encounter with the resurrected Christ,[306] wrote the

---
[303] Luke 24:1-6, 13-17
[304] Psalm 16, 22; Isaiah 53
[305] Mark 8:31, 9:30-31, 10:33-34
[306] Acts 9:1-9

majority of the New Testament. The entire book of Acts contains numerous appearances of the risen Christ to individuals and to large groups of people, and specific appearances to the disciples are located throughout the Synoptic Gospels as well.[307]

The first thing to take notice of is that the resurrection of Jesus was very special because it was a permanent resurrection into an imperishable, eternal body. The resurrected Jesus was the "first fruits"[308] of a novel paradigm of human life after death. This is *not* like Elijah raising a widow's son from the dead;[309] this is *not* like Elisha raising the Shunammite woman's son from the dead;[310] this is *not* like Lazarus being raised from the dead.[311] All of those people have died after coming back into temporal, perishable bodies. When Jesus rose from the dead, He had a transformed, glorified, immortal, flesh and bones [312] non-perishable body impervious to hunger, pain, suffering, death, and sickness.[313] And that physical body was very real, which is confirmed by the fact that the disciples touched Jesus's feet,[314] He took bread and broke it,[315] Thomas touched His hands and His side,[316] He made food,[317] and He ate and drank.[318]

Why Christ had to raise from the dead is very simple: "If Christ has not been raised, your faith is worthless; you are still in your sins."[319] In fact, the resurrection establishes Jesus as the only religious figure in the history of existence to have ever died and then come back from the dead to tell us about it.[320]

---

[307] Matthew 28:1-20; Mark 16:1-8; Luke 24:1-53; John 20:1-29
[308] I Corinthians 15:20, 23
[309] I Kings 17:17-24
[310] II Kings 4:18-37
[311] John 11:38-44
[312] Luke 24:39
[313] I Corinthians 15:42-44
[314] Matthew 28:9
[315] Luke 24:30
[316] John 20:27
[317] John 21:12-13
[318] Acts 10:41
[319] I Corinthians 15:17
[320] For more on circumstantial proofs of Jesus and the resurrection, I highly recommend *The Case for Christ* by Lee Strobel (Grand Rapids: Zondervan, 1998) or J.

From the standpoint of Christian doctrine, the resurrection has much significance. First, as believers, the resurrection regenerates all of us into new people being "born again" to a timeless hope through Christ.[321] We are made alive by Christ and raised up with Him,[322] so that we are continually putting to death our old sinful ways of being and living and in turn are considering ourselves alive to Christ.[323] As a result, we are no longer in bondage to sin,[324] and the Holy Spirit will empower the gospel to be spread to all who will hear.[325] This regeneration turned the original apostles who were fearful—and had abandoned Jesus before His resurrection—into bold men of faith who willingly died for the risen Lord. There is certainly something powerful and moving when the original disciples were willing to die for something they had seen with their own eyes.

Additionally, their paths to martyrdom were much less than glamorous. The resurrection turned skeptics and non-believers into devout followers of Christ, such as the conversion of Paul in Acts 9. It is worth noting that before Paul met the risen Christ, he made a name for himself persecuting and killing followers of Jesus. The resurrection revolutionized Jewish life and converted those Jewish followers of Jesus to, in many cases, instantaneously abandon thousands of years of tradition: they abandoned the law as a requirement for membership in the community, changed the Sabbath from Saturday to Sunday, ceased making animal sacrifices, and worshiped Jesus as Lord.[326] In the same line of thought, the celebration of communion and baptism in the early church (practices that still continue today) highlight the significance of the resurrection, because both symbolically celebrate the death and then rising up of Jesus. It defies logic for

---

N. D. Anderson's "The Evidence for the Resurrection" (London and Downers Grove, Ill: InterVarsity Press, 1966).
[321] I Peter 1:3
[322] Ephesians 2:5-6
[323] Romans 6:4-11
[324] Romans 6:14
[325] Acts 1:8
[326] *The Case for Christ* by Lee Strobel (Grand Rapids: Zondervan, 1998), 250-251.

anyone to *celebrate and cherish* someone's death unless that death meant something very, very significant. And the fact that Christianity as a new religion expanded and flourished under oppressive conditions to become what it is today testifies to the power of the resurrection.

Second, the resurrection of Christ justifies believers[327] so that there is no longer any penalty to pay for sin and no more wrath to endure from God. This is *not* a free pass to sin but rather an assurance, that we are all not ultimately fated to death because of sin. (Sanctification—a topic to be discussed in the second volume of *What Christians Should Know*—refers to the continuous, everyday, progressive molding of Christians to become more like Christ. It is an internal condition and a process that happens throughout our Christian lives. Believing in Christ, becoming saved and being justified happens at the start of our Christian lives.) *Only* by the power of the resurrected Christ can we become dead to sin and alive to Christ.[328] In fact, the resurrection also shows believers that the resurrection is what we all have to look forward to. Therefore, our labors on earth are not in vain,[329] because we know eventually we will be raised up[330] like Him into heaven.[331]

IV. Conclusion

What Christians should know is that the cross is *the* ultimate act of selfless love and sacrifice for the sake of others. So if you've ever wondered, "What has God done for me?" the answer is that He gave up everything, was rejected, tortured, suffered, and died for *your* sake.

Now that we have covered the core principles, I hope it has become very clear to all readers that what the Bible teaches is not a superficial, simple-minded, haphazard mess designed to

---

[327] Romans 4:25
[328] Romans 6:11
[329] I Corinthians 15:58
[330] I Thessalonians 4:17
[331] Luke 24:50-51; Acts 1:9-11

delude the ignorant and enslave the masses. It is an intellectually complex, rich, and enlightening Book to which no other "book" can compare.

Furthermore, the doctrine of Jesus Christ serves as *the* centerpiece of the Christian faith. Without Jesus, we have nothing, and we are nothing, because He holds the keys to everything. The Bible teaches us that Jesus lived and died for a specific purpose, and that purpose is very costly. It is only by God's grace that we are able to do anything. Never, ever make the mistake of thinking that God's grace is cheap.

"Cheap grace" justifies sin and never requires repentance. Cheap grace is granted *by us* and is given *for us*. God is never involved. As the great theologian Dietrich Bonhoeffer has written,

> Cheap grace is the preaching of forgiveness without requiring repentance, baptism without church discipline, Communion without confession, absolution without personal confession. Cheap grace is grace without discipleship, grace without the cross, grace without Jesus Christ ... Grace is *costly* because it calls us to follow, and it is grace because it calls us to follow *Jesus Christ*. It is costly because it costs a man his life, and it is grace because it gives a man the only true life. It is costly because it condemns sin, and grace because it justifies the sinner. Above all it is costly because it cost God the life of his Son: "ye were bought at a price," and what has cost God much cannot be cheap for us.[332]

And while Bonhoeffer's powerful words can illuminate the common fallacies of doctrine within the church, the power of Christ also reveals the inadequacies of other so-called religions as well.

Any form of polytheism fails because in such cases, there is no capital G "God" but many lowercase g "gods." Therefore, god isn't god at all but a subordinate line worker. Why would anyone ever worship something that is *not* worthy to be praised?

---

[332] Dietrich Bonhoeffer, *The Cost of Discipleship* (New York: Touchstone, 1959), 45.

Any institution, organization, or person that claims they hold the keys to the kingdom of heaven also fails miserably. Jesus is the perfect mediator, the perfect high priest, and *the* way to the Father. To suggest that a church or a clergy member takes Christ's place is heresy and is a tacit assertion that Christ isn't good enough and needs some help. True, in conversing with Peter in Matthew 16:18, Jesus says, "I also say to you that you are Peter, and upon this rock I will build My church; and the gates of Hades will not overpower it." But seven verses later in Matthew 16:23, Jesus says, "But He turned and said to Peter, 'Get behind Me, Satan! You are a stumbling block to Me; for you are not setting your mind on God's interests, but man's.'" One of the simplest messages the Bible teaches us is that casting a gaze on God always succeeds. Keeping our gaze on creation *always* fails and opens the door for Satan to walk right in.

Every other form of Monotheism, then, is an impotent, powerless religion based on non-truth and fruitless prescriptions. For example, the Law of Moses will save no one because no one is "justified by the works of the Law."[333] No form of "works" will save anyone, because if you can win God over on Judgment Day because you have more checks on your religion card than the next person, that effectively subjugates God to the works. Further, works does *absolutely nothing* to propitiate the wrath of God because of sin, nor does rule following pay the penalty *for* sin. In the Old Testament, animal sacrifices used to be a temporizing measure, but such practices were never adequate, nor did they *atone* for sin.[334]

If someone were to simply say that God can "just forgive" sin, then I would agree, but the God of the Bible is also just, so He may forgive sin but a price must be paid because of His justice. If God simply says, "Never mind" to sin, then He is *not* righteous and can thus invite every cruel, perverse, wicked, and malicious individual to fellowship with him with a casual shrug of the shoulders.

---

[333] Galatians 2:16; cf. Romans 3:20
[334] Hebrews 10:1-10

Any faith that excludes the historical person of Jesus and the historical event of the resurrection therefore admits that there can be no propitiation, no atonement, no justification, no sanctification, and no eternal life. Without Jesus there is only one option: death.

CHAPTER VI
COVENANT

A covenant is an agreement that is imposed by God between Himself and human beings based upon a core ethos: "I will put My law within them and on their heart I will write it; and I will be their God, and they shall be My people."[335] Within the covenant are certain stipulations that specify covenantal obligations. If one remains faithful and keeps the commandments, that person will receive many blessings. If one does not obey the commandments, that person will face adverse consequences.

The reason God initiates covenants is for the purpose of relationship—He wants to have a connection with us, and a covenant is intended to strengthen the bond between two parties. A covenant is an undeserved, free gift from a loving Father for His children. In essence, God is showing us how we should act by Him first making promises about how He will act toward us—and those promises are trustworthy because God is unchangeable and cannot lie.[336] Therefore, all covenants are unalterable, and we cannot negotiate with God in order to change the terms of the agreement. We are free to either accept the terms or to reject them.

Covenants are built upon *mutual trust*, whereas contracts are built upon *mutual distrust*. In a covenant, God wants to give and wants to provide, and so He gives of Himself for our sake. On the other hand, you sign a contract in order to protect *your* interests, now that you are forced and *have* to do something. A contract also typically involves taking away: you give something

---

[335] Jeremiah 31:33
[336] For a complete lesson on God's characteristics, please see Chapter II.

up in order to get something. In a covenant, God gives us everything.

Let us all not forget that God needs nothing and therefore never had to make any covenant, but He did. Covenants are purely voluntary and initiated by Him out of the love He has for creation. God essentially is "putting Himself out there" and invites us into relationship with Him, and that relationship bears the gift of many promises if we choose to obey and follow the conditions of the covenant. *We* can go back on our word and violate the terms of the covenant. In essence, we have everything to gain and God has everything to lose. Just think about the last time you came to an agreement with someone, and they did not keep up their end of the deal. How did you feel? Did you want to take revenge? Did you want to give them a piece of your mind? Now, imagine if that same person fails on their end over, and over, and over again. That's how God feels, but *in spite of this*, He keeps on keeping on and remains faithful to what He said He would do.

In *Systematic Theology*, Wayne Grudem refers to covenants by writing, "The Greek translators of the Old Testament [and] the New Testament authors did not use the ordinary Greek word for contracts or agreements in which both parties were equal (*syntheke*), but rather chose a less common word, *diatheke*, which emphasized that the provisions of the covenant were laid down by one of the parties only."[337]

In this lesson, we will discuss the covenants between God and human beings, but covenants also do exist between human beings as well. For example, marriage is considered a covenant when a man and a woman become one.[338] The Biblical ideal of a marriage is two people loving and serving one another with a unified gaze on God. It is meant to be a selfless, other-serving, unbreakable bond. Parenting is another example, in which the mother and father continuously give to their children out of love. And the covenant of parenting is an ideal example of how God

---

[337] Wayne Grudem, *Systematic Theology* (Grand Rapids: Zondervan, 1994), 515.
[338] Genesis 2:24; Malachi 2:14-16; Matthew 19:3-6; Ephesians 5:33

relates to us, because no matter how bad your children are, no matter what they do, they will always be your children, and you will always be their parent. Nothing can ever change that, and you will always pursue and care for them just as God will always pursue us, always love us, and is unable to turn His back on us.

A covenant is comprised of four specific criteria: (1) *Parties* who are involved in the covenant other than God. Typically, a person serves as a representative in the covenant for everyone else. (2) *Provisions and Conditions* that stipulate the terms of the relationship and consequences for violating the covenant. (3) *Promises* and blessings for obedience and how one can obtain those blessings. Some covenants also have a (4) *Picture*: a sign that represents the covenant. This sign can be external, internal, or both. The following covenants are presented in order as they appear in the Bible. They are not separate from one another but build atop one another.

I. The Adamic Covenant

The Adamic Covenant reveals that since our beginning, God's relationship to us has been defined by specific stipulations. The Adamic covenant is outlined in Genesis 1:27-30 and 2:16-17. Of note, the text in Genesis never refers to a "covenant," but Hosea does refer to the sins of Israel and writes in 6:7, "But like Adam they have transgressed the covenant."

In Genesis 1:27-30, the Bible says, "God created man in His own image, in the image of God He created him; male and female He created them. God blessed them; and God said to them, 'Be fruitful and multiply, and fill the earth, and subdue it; and rule over the fish of the sea and over the birds of the sky and over every living thing that moves on the earth.' Then God said, 'Behold, I have given you every plant yielding seed that is on the surface of all the earth, and every tree which has fruit yielding seed; it shall be food for you; and to every beast of the earth and to every bird of the sky and to every thing that moves on the earth which has life, I have given every green plant for food'; and it was so."

Genesis 2:16-17 then says, "The LORD God commanded the man, saying, 'From any tree of the garden you may eat freely; but from the tree of the knowledge of good and evil you shall not eat, for in the day that you eat from it you will surely die.'"

Parties: Adam as a representative of all humankind.[339]

Provisions and Conditions: The text in Genesis tells us that God blessed Adam and provided him with the earth, the Garden of Eden, his wife, Eve, and dominion over the creatures of the earth. Through the Garden, He gave Adam free food and a place to live. These provisions came with the condition that no one was to eat from the tree of knowledge of good and evil. The consequence for this violation was death.

Promise: By implication, before the Fall, Adam and Eve would have had eternal life eating from the tree of life.[340] After the Fall, God ultimately promised that Jesus would crush the serpent.[341] Because of sin, Adam and Eve could not have remained in the Garden, because they would have then been able to eat from the tree of life and dwell eternally in their fallen state. The promise of Jesus is of so much importance because before Adam and Eve take one step outside of Eden, God has already laid the plans for Jesus to save everyone, which means everything in the Bible that is going to happen before the birth of Jesus points *directly* to Christ.

Picture: The "sign" for the Adamic covenant isn't as clear cut as the other components. Essentially, in this covenant, God voluntarily enters into a relationship with Adam and gives him many gifts. Adam and God are now inseparably bound together, signified by the union of Adam and Eve (i.e., marriage) and two now becoming one.[342] A more tangible sign would be the tree of life in the Garden of Eden, representing God's promise of eternal life. In addition, in regards to the Sabbath, "God blessed the

---

[339] Romans 5:12-21
[340] Genesis 3:22
[341] Genesis 3:15
[342] Genesis 2:24

seventh day and sanctified it, because in it He rested from all His work which God had created and made" (Genesis 2:3).

Note also that God chose humans as the only part of creation with whom to have a covenant. For example, God did not initiate a covenant with plants or animals.

II. The Noahic Covenant

The setup: Many generations pass between Adam and Noah, and things aren't looking so good for humanity. Everyone on the face of the earth is doing evil, and the Bible says in Genesis 6:5-9 that humankind's wickedness grieved the LORD. God had already made a promise to Adam to have dominion over creation, so God can't wipe all of creation out. Instead, He chooses Noah (who found favor in God's eyes)[343] to build an ark to survive the flood that will blot out the corruption of humankind. God then makes this covenant with Noah after he, his family, and many kinds of animals leave the ark and are back on dry land.

In Genesis 9:8-17, it says, "Then God spoke to Noah and to his sons with him, saying, 'Now behold, I Myself do establish My covenant with you, and with your descendants after you; and with every living creature that is with you, the birds, the cattle, and every beast of the earth with you; of all that comes out of the ark, even every beast of the earth. I establish My covenant with you; and all flesh shall never again be cut off by the water of the flood, neither shall there again be a flood to destroy the earth.' God said, 'This is the sign of the covenant which I am making between Me and you and every living creature that is with you, for all successive generations; I set My bow in the cloud, and it shall be for a sign of a covenant between Me and the earth. It shall come about, when I bring a cloud over the earth, that the bow will be seen in the cloud, and I will remember My covenant, which is between Me and you and every living creature of all flesh; and never again shall the water become a flood to destroy

---

[343] Genesis 6:8

all flesh. When the bow is in the cloud, then I will look upon it, to remember the everlasting covenant between God and every living creature of all flesh that is on the earth.' And God said to Noah, 'This is the sign of the covenant which I have established between Me and all flesh that is on the earth.'"

Parties: Noah and all his descendants along with every living thing on Earth. God initiated this covenant with Noah *as a function of God's grace.*

Provisions and Conditions: God blesses Noah and his sons, and He commands them all to be fruitful and multiply in Genesis 9:1. God also says in 9:3 that "'every moving thing that is alive shall be food for you; I give all to you, as I gave the green plant.'" These provisions come with the condition that the value of life, especially human life, be honored. Anyone who does not value human life is held accountable to God.[344]

Promise: An unconditional, divine guarantee to never again destroy life on Earth with a flood. Jesus is the ultimate promise of the Noahic covenant, as He is the one who saves us from God's judgment through faith.

Picture: The rainbow. The symbolism, of course, of the bow being in the clouds is that if it is up there, it can't be used for war. By Noah *and his sons* being blessed, the image of a blessed community of family members begins to emerge.

III. The Abrahamic Covenant

The setup: Many generations pass between Noah and Abraham. The Bible introduces us to Abram in Genesis 11:26, and then in Genesis 12:1-3, God commands him, and he obeys. Once again, God chooses a human being based upon His divine initiative. In fact, the command that God gives Abram in 12:1-3 foreshadows the covenant.

---

[344] Genesis 9:4-7

There are two parts to the Abrahamic Covenant from Genesis 15:9-21 and chapter 17.

Genesis 15:18 says, "On that day the LORD made a covenant with Abram, saying, 'To your descendants I have given this land, from the river of Egypt as far as the great river, the river Euphrates.'"

Genesis 17:7 says, "'I will establish My covenant between Me and you and your descendants after you throughout their generations for an everlasting covenant, to be God to you and to your descendants after you.'"

Parties: Abraham (God renames him this from Abram in this covenant). God chose Abraham, and Abraham had faith, and that faith was reckoned to him as righteousness.[345]

Promises, Provisions, and Conditions: A divine guarantee to grant Abraham land, sons, and to be the father of a "multitude of nations."[346] (The land is Canaan.) God also promises to conditionally be the God of Abraham if he and his descendants are obedient to the LORD. God requires that Abraham be "blameless"[347] and that all of his descendants also keep the covenant that God has made with him. God specifically tells Abraham that his wife, Sarah, will bear a child whom he will call Isaac, and God will continue His covenant through him and his descendants. Through the seed of Abraham, blessings will subsequently come to the entire world, and this was based upon total consecration to God. Jesus is the ultimate promise of the Abrahamic covenant as the one Man who brings blessings to the entire world for all those who have faith in Him.

Picture: The external sign was circumcision. The text further stipulates that any male who was not circumcised would be "cut off from the people."[348] The internal sign was faith. By Abraham,

---

[345] Genesis 15:6
[346] Genesis 17:4
[347] Genesis 17:1
[348] Genesis 17:14

his sons, and the land (although yet to be occupied) being blessed, the image of a blessed nation begins to emerge.

IV. The Mosaic Covenant (or the Sinaitic Covenant)

The setup: Abraham has a son, Isaac. Isaac has a son, Jacob. Jacob has 12 sons and number 11 is named Joseph. Joseph becomes a very big deal in Egypt, and the family that was living in Canaan moves to Egypt. Many generations pass and what was a family of less than 100 turns into "Israel," an Egyptian subclass but soon-to-be nation of many, many people. God calls Moses and says, "You're up. Time to set My people free." Moses obeys, and he tells Pharaoh, "Let my people go." Ten plagues hit Egypt, and then finally Pharaoh lets the people go after the tenth plague, when all the firstborn in Egypt die, except those in houses marked with the blood of an unblemished lamb on the doorposts and lintel. God *passed over* those houses. Now, Moses is leading all the Egyptian exiles in the wilderness. God then visits Mount Sinai and speaks directly to Moses and gives him "the Law," including the 10 Commandments. In total, the Mosaic Law has over 600 commandments.

The source for this covenant comes from Exodus 19-24.

Exodus 20:1-3 says, "Then God spoke all these words, saying, 'I am the LORD your God, who brought you out of the land of Egypt, out of the house of slavery. You shall have no other gods before Me.'"

Exodus 24:1-8 says, "Then He said to Moses, 'Come up to the LORD, you and Aaron, Nadab and Abihu and seventy of the elders of Israel, and you shall worship at a distance. Moses alone, however, shall come near to the LORD, but they shall not come near, nor shall the people come up with him.' Then Moses came and recounted to the people all the words of the LORD and all the ordinances; and all the people answered with one voice and said, 'All the words which the LORD has spoken we will do!' Moses wrote down all the words of the LORD. Then he arose early in the morning, and built an altar at the foot of the mountain with twelve pillars for the twelve tribes of Israel. He sent young men of the sons of Israel, and they offered burnt offerings and sacrificed young bulls as peace offerings to the LORD. Moses took half of the blood and put *it* in basins, and the *other* half of the blood he sprinkled on the altar. Then he took the book of the covenant and read *it* in the hearing of the people; and they said, 'All that the LORD has spoken we will do, and we will be obedient!' So Moses took the blood and sprinkled *it* on the people, and said, 'Behold the blood of the covenant, which the LORD has made with you in accordance with all these words.'"

Parties: Moses serves as the mediator between God and the people of Israel. Israel is comprised of all those God freed from Egyptian bondage, who are the descendants of Abraham. It becomes clear then, how this covenant stacks on top of the Abrahamic covenant. Note that God frees the people *first* and then invites them to enter into covenant with Him.

Provisions and Conditions: God makes a conditional divine pledge to be the God of Israel, to protect her and to safeguard her blessings so long as the people execute total consecration to God, serve Him, and obey His commandments. These conditions are specifically laid out as the Mosaic Law, and the first part of the Law are the 10 Commandments written by God Himself on two stone tablets. By obeying and keeping the Law, the people will maintain their freedom from earthly powers.

Promise: Jesus is the ultimate promise of the Mosaic covenant as the One who mediates for us to deliver us from bondage, the One who ultimately fulfills the law, and the One whose atoning blood saves us from wrath and judgment. In other words, Christ's blood causes God to pass over us.

Picture: The external sign of this covenant was the Passover in Egypt (Exodus 12). This is why God begins in Exodus 20 saying (I will summarize and paraphrase), "Hey guys, remember how I saved all your firstborn from death in Egypt? That was me. That was me giving you a friendly reminder that I am God and you are my people." Of course, the people and Moses had to believe (faith) in God in order to follow His law. By Israel being set apart and blessed, the image emerges of a *holy* nation, separated from the rest, who serve God alone.

V. The Davidic Covenant

The setup: Israel wanders in the desert some more and eventually enters the Promised Land. The people face constant enemies and skirmishes, but over time they grow into a nation. Yet, for quite some time, they have no king to rule over all of Israel. The people chose the first king, Saul, and things would end very poorly for him. But God had already called the prophet Samuel to anoint the young shepherd boy, David, to be Israel's next king. In II Samuel 7, David is ruling from Jerusalem (the capital) and is experiencing a rare time of rest in his kingship. David *thinks* he should build a house in which God could "dwell," but the LORD responds in one of the most beautiful passages in the entire Bible.

II Samuel 7:5-16 says, "'Go and say to My servant David, "Thus says the LORD, 'Are you the one who should build Me a house to dwell in? For I have not dwelt in a house since the day I brought up the sons of Israel from Egypt, even to this day; but I have been moving about in a tent, even in a tabernacle. Wherever I have gone with all the sons of Israel, did I speak a word with one of the tribes of Israel, which I commanded to shepherd My people Israel, saying, "Why have you not built Me a house of cedar?"'" Now therefore, thus you shall say to My servant David, "Thus says the LORD of hosts, 'I took you from the pasture, from following the sheep, to be ruler over My people Israel. I have been with you wherever you have gone and have cut off all your enemies from before you; and I will make you a great name, like the names of the great men who are on the earth. I will also appoint a place for My people Israel and will plant them, that they may live in their own place and not be disturbed again, nor will the wicked afflict them any more as formerly, even from the day that I commanded judges to be over My people Israel; and I will give you rest from all your enemies.

The LORD also declares to you that the LORD will make a house for you. When your days are complete and you lie down with your fathers, I will raise up your descendant after you, who will come forth from you, and I will establish his kingdom. He shall build a house for My name, and I will establish the throne of his kingdom forever. I will be a father to him and he will be a son to Me; when he commits iniquity, I will correct him with the rod of men and the strokes of the sons of men, but My lovingkindness shall not depart from him, as I took *it* away from Saul, whom I removed from before you. Your house and your kingdom shall endure before Me forever; your throne shall be established forever.'"

Parties: David, referred to as a "servant" of the LORD (also by implication the people).

Provisions and Conditions: God will finally give the people rest and locate the people in their "own place." He will also make David great and a ruler over God's people. The conditions of the covenant are that sin has consequences, and when sin is committed, the rod of correction will be used.

Promises: Essentially, the promise is a King of Kings who shall have an eternal kingdom. The Davidic Covenant is an unconditional divine pledge to establish and maintain the dynasty of king David forever, and to bring the dynasty into rest inside the Promised Land. It becomes clear that Jesus is the ultimate promise of the Davidic covenant as the One who will have an eternal dynasty.[349]

Picture: David had faith (internal sign) in God. That commitment was externalized as a Temple that would be built not by David, but by his son, Solomon. Symbolically, a kingdom that David's line rules over serves as a metaphor for the covenant.

A bit more on the Davidic Covenant: This covenant follows the Ancient Near East tradition of a "royal grant." Royal grants were normally initiated by a king toward a servant in reward for

---

[349] Luke 1:33

some form of outstanding service. Such grants typically were ongoing and unconditional, and the heirs of the faithful servant also reaped the benefits of the grant so long as they remained in service, loyal, and faithful. This form of covenant is promissory and not obligatory.

King David is described at a time of peace when he was "settled in his house" and "the Lord had given him rest from all his enemies around him." From this imperial sense of peace, and perhaps inspired by political might, the king declares *his* own initiative to build a temple to honor God. While the intent is honorable, one must also recognize the self-interest present in this declaration: at the time, one of the most potent symbols to define, legitimize, and solidify rule was to build a temple. Hence, by creating a place where God would "live," David also acts to solidify his crown. God subsequently responds to the human gesture by asking, "Are you the one to build me a house to live in?" As Walter Brueggeman says, "The temple guarantees God's presence but at the same time militates against God's freedom."[350] In short, God excels past the boundaries of the material world, and even a "house of cedar" is not luxurious enough to contain His majesty. Notably at this point in chapter 7, *God* has not yet spoken.

When God does respond, the LORD does not rebuke or chastise His servant for self-interest or self-directed building projects. Rather, through Nathan, the Lord reminds the king of God's gracious favor and all that has been done for Israel, starting with liberation from Egyptian bondage to the present, and raising up David from humble shepherd beginnings to sit on the throne of Israel. Then, after this reminder of a gracious past, the LORD establishes the continuity of grace from then to the future. God begins in verse 8 by saying "I took you," highlighting the divine hand in David's rise and emphasizing that it is Him, not David, who is the ultimate first cause of *all* things.

---

[350] Walter Brueggemann, *Interpretation: A Bible Commentary for Teaching and Preaching: First and Second Samuel* (Louisville: Westminster John Knox Press, 2012), 254.

The LORD builds upon history by then offering unwarranted, unmerited promises: "I will make for you a great name ... I will appoint a place ... I will give you rest."

The promise of God comes to a peak in verse 11, when the Lord declares that, "the LORD will make you a house." This is a play on words: the Hebrew word *baiyt*, can refer to a physical family house but is also used in a broader sense to refer to a dynasty.[351] David had used the same term in order to build God a *baiyt*, yet in spite of this, God responds to David's inability to fashion a container (temple) for The Almighty by promising an even greater free gift that cannot be contained (a dynasty). In essence, God responds to David's temporary solution by offering a permanent, everlasting social reality that will be enjoyed by generations to come.

Arguably, these verses in II Samuel 7 lay the foundation of Biblical faith for the entire Bible—that God has provided an unconditional promise and free gift to all, and our faith is contingent upon that unmerited favor; no matter what we as human beings do, and no matter how we turn away from Him, the Lord will continually pour out His steadfast love over us.

With prior *conditional* covenants, violation of the stipulations could result in forfeiture of God's promise. Now, God has put Himself on the line and made His promise *unconditional*, typified by the use of the word "but" (as in, "but, *in spite of this*") in verse 15, and the now permanent obligation never to "take my steadfast love from him." No longer are we held in bondage by the law and the myriad of conditional "if" requirements set forth in the Mosaic Covenant. And it is God, though Christ (eventually), that will ultimately fulfill the law so that nothing any human can ever do will make God turn His back on us.

VI. The New Covenant

The setup: David and Solomon rule over a united Israel, but once Solomon dies, the kingdom falls apart and is split into two:

---

[351] Ibid, 255.

Israel is in the North and Judah is in the South. For the most part, the successive kings that rule over each half of the nation are evil and apostate, and countless prophets basically tell the people, "If you don't shape up, God is going to deal with you." The people do not listen, and as a result, the Assyrians conquer Israel and the people are exiled. Judah is conquered by the Babylonians and the people are exiled. Jeremiah is a prophet who speaks about the impending Babylonian crisis.

In Jeremiah 31:31-34 it says, "'Behold, days are coming,' declares the LORD, 'when I will make a new covenant with the house of Israel and with the house of Judah, not like the covenant which I made with their fathers in the day I took them by the hand to bring them out of the land of Egypt, My covenant which they broke, although I was a husband to them,' declares the LORD. 'But this is the covenant which I will make with the house of Israel after those days,' declares the LORD, 'I will put My law within them and on their heart I will write it; and I will be their God, and they shall be My people. They will not teach again, each man his neighbor and each man his brother, saying, "Know the LORD," for they will all know Me, from the least of them to the greatest of them,' declares the LORD, 'for I will forgive their iniquity, and their sin I will remember no more.'"

Parties: Ultimately, the mediator of this covenant is Jesus.

Provisions and Conditions: God provides the apostate Israel with this covenant on the verge of the people being exiled from the Promised Land for covenantal violation.[352] Essentially, this covenant offers endless provision, because it's the covenant that keeps on giving. From the forgiveness of sins, humanity derives salvation, regeneration, eternal life, fellowship with God, sanctification, and illumination, just to name a few perks. The condition for this covenant is having faith in Jesus and to follow the law written on one's heart.

Promise: An unconditional divine pledge of pure grace. Because Israel was continually unfaithful, God makes the decision to

---

[352] Leviticus 26:27-39; Deuteronomy 28:36-37, 45-68

forgive her sins and establish a new relationship where the law is no longer external but written on their hearts. God will forgive sins and remember them no more. As a result, the apex of the new promise is that everyone who has faith and obeys will have eternal life and fellowship with God.[353] This promise is only possible through Jesus.

Picture: The internal sign of the New Covenant is faith. The external signs are baptism and communion. Baptism, then, represents the *start* of the covenant. Communion represents the *continuance* of the covenant.

In order to put the New Covenant in context, let us look to the New Testament in Matthew 26:26-29: "While they were eating, Jesus took some bread, and after a blessing, He broke it and gave it to the disciples, and said, 'Take, eat; this is My body.' And when He had taken a cup and given thanks, He gave it to them, saying, 'Drink from it, all of you; *for this is My blood of the covenant*, which is poured out for many for forgiveness of sins. But I say to you, I will not drink of this fruit of the vine from now on until that day when I drink it new with you in My Father's kingdom'" (italics mine).

Jesus said these words to His disciples as they ate the Passover meal.[354] And this passage is located in the book of Matthew, written by a disciple largely concerned with how Jesus is the fulfillment of the Old Testament, where all of the prior covenants are recorded.

Essentially, since the beginning in Genesis, humans were unable to obtain the blessings offered in all of the covenants because they were incapable of meeting the conditions. So, it became necessary for God to graciously give more in order to save His creation. As is always the case, humans can't do, so God does and provides. The entire impetus behind covenants is revealed as God miraculously working out a plan of redemption

---

[353] John 3:15, 5:24
[354] Matthew 26:17-19

for sinful people. It is God's *hesed*, or unmerited grace, that makes all of this possible.

So in the New Covenant, Christ now becomes a mediator[355] for us *between* humanity and the Father, because in the past, a covenant directly between God and humans failed. Just as in every other covenant, in order to participate in this covenant, one ought to have faith[356] and believe in Christ as the One who redeems humanity. This models every other covenant in the Bible, because in order for it to work, the person had to believe in and trust in God. Also, in prior covenants, the people involved were incapable of obedience because they lacked the redemption and atoning sacrifice of Jesus Christ, who now frees us from the bondage of sin,[357] which prevents us from obeying God. With the New Covenant, faith produces obedience,[358] and thus we become participants in the promise.[359] And this covenantal promise is *everlasting* with *everyone* who believes, so that God will be your God, you shall be His,[360] the Holy Spirit works in us to bring about New Covenant power,[361] and God is subsequently revealed to us in full.[362]

A valid question to ask is if there is a "new covenant," then what is the "old covenant"? The new *is the replacement*[363] of the old Mosaic covenant and is the fulfillment of every other Old Testament covenant.[364] In some instances, writers of the New Testament refer to the Mosaic Covenant as the "old,"[365] and the reason this old covenant existed in the first place was to point people toward Christ.[366] Galatians 3:24 says, "Therefore the Law

---

[355] Hebrews 8:6, 9:15, 12:24
[356] Romans 1:17, 5:1
[357] Romans 8:2
[358] James 2:17
[359] I John 2:4-6
[360] Jeremiah 32:38-40; Ezekiel 34:30-31, 36:28; II Corinthians 6:16; I Peter 2:9-10; Revelation 21:3
[361] Acts 1:8; I Corinthians 12:13; II Corinthians 3:4-18
[362] John 1:14; Hebrews 1:1-3
[363] Luke 22:20; I Corinthians 11:25; II Corinthians 3:6; Hebrews 8:8, 13, 9:15, 12:24
[364] Luke 1:72-73; Romans 4; Galatians 3:6-18, 29; Hebrews 2:16, 6:13-20
[365] II Corinthians 3:14; Hebrews 8:6,13
[366] Galatians 3:19

has become our tutor to lead us to Christ, so that we may be justified by faith." Furthermore, the book of Hebrews makes it clear that because the Mosaic Covenant does not take away sins,[367] it points directly toward Christ, who is the perfect high priest and the ultimate atoning sacrifice.[368] The Mosaic Covenant frustrates people and forces them to say, "This is too hard. I can't do it by myself. There must be a better way." That better way is Jesus. If the Mosaic Covenant *could* yield righteousness and could give eternal life, then Christ would not be necessary.[369]

Christ fulfills the Adamic Covenant by fully obeying God's commands, and through Him (instead of eating from a tree), all who have faith will have eternal life. Christ fulfills the Noahic Covenant in that He is the One who is righteous and saves us from the judgment of God due to sin. He is the ark that protects us and keeps us safe. The flood, or the baptism of the world, re-creates creation in order to reconcile us back to God, and Christ mediates this process. Christ fulfills the Abrahamic Covenant as He is the blessed descendant of Abraham.[370] Jesus was also circumcised in the Jewish tradition and fully obeyed all of God's commands, thus fulfilling the Mosaic Covenant. And because of His total consecration to God, blessings come to the entire world. Christ fulfills the Davidic Covenant as the eternal King whose dynasty and kingdom shall endure forever. It's all about Jesus, all the time.

For Further Study

Walter Brueggemann and Tod Linafelt, *An Introduction to the Old Testament* (Louisville, KY: Westminster John Knox Press, 2003).

---

[367] Hebrews 10:1-4
[368] Hebrews 9:11-28
[369] Galatians 3:21
[370] Matthew 1:1-17

CHAPTER VII
GRACE AND STEWARDSHIP

I. Grace

In *On the Grace of God*, Justin Holcomb writes, "'Grace' is the most important concept in the Bible, in Christianity, and in the world. It is most clearly expressed in the promise of God revealed in Scripture and embodied in Jesus Christ. The deepest message of the ministry of Jesus and of the entire Bible is the grace of God to sinners and sufferers."[371]

What Christians should know is that grace simply refers to the unmerited favor that God grants to us all.

As sinners, we deserve nothing, are unworthy of the LORD'S favor, are unrighteous by our own works, and have proven ourselves unfit to receive the unconditional love of God. Yet, in spite of all of this, God freely reaches down and picks us up—even those who spite Him. Isaiah 55:7 says:

> "Let the wicked forsake his way
> And the unrighteous man his thoughts;
> And let him return to the LORD,
> And He will have compassion on him,
> And to our God,
> For He will abundantly pardon."

By our own warrant, humankind deserves only judgment, but God executes mercy and does not consider merit. Therefore, grace not only entails getting what you *don't* merit, it also entails *not* receiving what you *do* merit. Non-believers often chastise God by pointing to all the evil in the world, and therefore say, "God is unjust, cruel and mean." What they often neglect to

---

[371] Justin S. Holcomb, *On the Grace of God* (Wheaton, IL: Crossway, 2013), 11.

realize is that it is *only* by God's gracious favor that He does not unleash the wrath that we rightfully deserve because of sin. Matthew 5:45 says that God "causes His sun to rise on the evil and the good and sends rain on the righteous and the unrighteous." In fact, God is patient and waits for people to repent, because He derives no joy in seeing people perish.[372] Thankfully for us, mercy triumphs over judgment.[373] If God were not so tremendously gracious, then existence would be impossible due to the utter depravity and destructiveness of sin.[374] If God were not so tremendously gracious, then anytime anyone mocks God or dehumanizes another person, judgment would be immediate and swift.

For the sake of simplicity in this lesson, I will refer to grace in a general sense, but it will become clear to any diligent student of doctrine that theologians and Bible scholars have delineated many different "types" of grace that typically refer to *the audience* and *the effects* of the grace. Here, I am more concerned with the principle of grace itself as opposed to its application to specific cohorts in specific scenarios. God is unchanging and thus consistently gracious in and of Himself, yet that grace is manifested to us in different ways. God is gracious to everyone in order to redeem those who will be saved,[375] to reveal His kindness and compassion,[376] and to reveal His justice.[377] Romans 2:5 and 3:19 say that on the final Day of Judgment, God will basically show everyone how ungracious they have been and reveal how gracious He has been *in spite of* their unfaithfulness. As a result, "every mouth may be closed and all the world may become accountable to God."

Psalm 145:8-9 says, "The LORD is gracious and merciful;

Slow to anger and great in lovingkindness. The LORD is good to all, And His mercies are over all His works." Hence, the LORD

---

[372] II Peter 3:9
[373] James 2:13
[374] For a full discussion of sin and its consequences, please refer to Chapter IV.
[375] II Peter 3:9-10
[376] Ezekiel 33:11; I Timothy 2:4
[377] Romans 2:5, 3:19

is not gracious to *some* people but to *all* people, even to those who reject Him. Because they deny Him, many people will voluntarily refuse the invitation by grace to have faith, trust in Jesus, repent, be regenerated, become sanctified, and ultimately live eternally with God—all results that would happen *if* they accepted the same grace that saves everyone else.

The apostle Paul described the gospel as "the gospel of the grace of God."[378] He also described God's grace as abundant,[379] sufficient,[380] and rich.[381] The theologian John Calvin called grace "gratuitous," referring to a gift that is sovereign, unearned, uncalled for, lacking good reason, and done free of charge. Calvin says, "We make the foundation of faith the gratuitous promise, because in it faith properly consists … Faith begins with the promise, rests in it, and ends in it."[382] Of course, the gratuitous promise is Jesus Christ, the ultimate expression of the grace of God.[383]

Grace flows from God to us. That current is never reversed. When a person says, "I'm a nobody," grace says, "You're a somebody." When a person says, "I'm worthless," grace says, "You're a child of God." When a person says, "I have nothing," God's grace says, "Here, have some more." When a person says, "I am too broken to amount to anything. There is no hope," God says, "Out of nothing I made everything.[384] Now imagine what I can do with you."

Gratuitous grace equals unconditional love and points directly to the idea that our salvation is a function of God's grace alone through faith alone.[385] If this were not the case, then we, as

---

[378] Acts 20:24
[379] Romans 5:15, 17, 20; II Corinthians 9:8; I Timothy 1:14
[380] II Corinthians 12:9
[381] II Corinthians 9:14; Ephesians 1:7, 2:7
[382] John Calvin, *Institutes of the Christian Religion*, ed. J. T. McNeil, trans. Ford Lewis Battles (Philadelphia: Westminster, 1960), 3.2.24.
[383] John 1:17, 3:16; Romans 5:6; Revelation 22:21
[384] Genesis 1:1-31
[385] Ephesians 2:8-9. For more on the cardinal doctrine of salvation being by grace alone and through faith alone, please refer to Chapter V.

sinners, could "earn" God's favor. Gratuitous grace destroys religious elitism (Pharisaism) or spiritual pride, because no one is "better" or "more special" than anyone else: all have fallen short of God's glory.[386] In fact, grace represents a paradigm of inversion that uplifts those that are oppressed.[387] Anyone is free to ask for God's grace at any time,[388] but we are all undeserving and receive grace as a function of nothing that *we* do—only God decides to whom He gives grace.[389] If works did play a role in grace, then it would no longer be grace.[390] It is this fact that God can be graceful to those who don't deserve it that makes the gospel of Jesus Christ so powerful. Without grace, we would all be doomed to one certain fate: death.

The Hebrew word for grace, *hesed*, is frequently used in the Old Testament.[391] It means "goodness, kindness, and faithfulness." *Hesed* frees people from bondage,[392] is slow to anger and abounds in steadfast love,[393] and is even demonstrated to those who will ultimately reject God;[394] hence, *hesed* is not conditional on our response. Grace overflows to all people,[395] enables people to therefore trust in God (faith),[396] and facilitates repentance.[397] The grace of God works in us so that we receive the gospel and bear fruit,[398] and by grace, the Holy Spirit works in us to will and work for God's pleasure.[399] Grace allows us to excel in everything,[400] forgives iniquity and heals ailments,[401] permits us to

---

[386] Romans 3:20-24
[387] Matthew 9:12, 20:28; Mark 2:17, 10:45; Luke 4:18-19, 5:31, 6:20-26
[388] Psalm 123:3; Isaiah 30:19; Malachi 1:9
[389] Exodus 33:19
[390] Romans 11:6
[391] Especially the Psalms. For example: 25:6, 40:11, 51:1, 69:16, 103:4.
[392] Exodus 12
[393] Exodus 34:6-7
[394] Mark 4:1-20
[395] Luke 3:6; Acts 2:17, 21; Titus 2:11
[396] Acts 14:3, 26, 15:40, 18:27, 20:24, 32.
[397] Acts 5:31, 11:18
[398] Colossians 1:6; II Peter 1:3-9
[399] Ephesians 2:10; Philippians 2:13
[400] II Corinthians 8:7
[401] Psalm 103:1-22

endure hardship,[402] justifies us,[403] strengthens our hearts,[404] and regenerates us into new people.[405] Grace permits favorable environmental conditions,[406] blesses those around faithful servants of God,[407] intellectually enlightens people,[408] and gives everyone a sense of right and wrong in our consciences.[409] *Everything* in our Christian walk is dependant on grace: who we are,[410] what we do,[411] how we act toward others,[412] how we live,[413] what we say,[414] where we derive our strength,[415] where we gain our sense of contentment,[416] and how we respond to the ills of life.[417]

Regeneration (see Chapter IX) refers to being made spiritually alive in Christ Jesus. Regeneration is an act of grace. If a person is spiritually dead and rejects God, that person obviously cannot benefit from the saving grace of God working in their life. In order to be raised and enter into a new life, we all have to be "born again" and raised from spiritual death by Jesus. We are incapable of raising ourselves from the dead, but God can. Hence, without being born again, no one can see God's kingdom.[418] As an example, I invite everyone to read the passage on Lazarus,[419] who was raised from the dead by the command of Christ. At the end of the story in John 11:44, it says, "The man who had died came forth, bound hand and foot with wrappings, and his face was wrapped around with a cloth. Jesus said to them, 'Unbind him, and

---

[402] II Corinthians 12:9
[403] Romans 3:24
[404] Hebrews 13:9
[405] II Corinthians 5:17
[406] Acts 14:16-17
[407] Genesis 39:5
[408] John 1:9
[409] Romans 2:14-15
[410] I Corinthians 15:10
[411] II Corinthians 2:12
[412] I Peter 4:10
[413] Romans 5:17; I Peter 3:7
[414] Colossians 4:6
[415] II Timothy 2:1
[416] II Corinthians 9:8
[417] I Peter 5:10
[418] John 3:3
[419] John 11. See also the resurrection of the widow's son in Luke 7:11-17.

let him go.'" In other words, the man who was "bound" to death was set free to live by the grace and power of Jesus Christ.

Augustine once said that, "What God's grace has not freed will not be free."[420] Without God's grace, it is impossible for us to break the chains of bondage. It is simply *because* we are the workmanship of the LORD and created in Christ Jesus for good works[421] that we ought to walk in the path of the original workman. Our behavior thus originates from our identity, and that identity is rooted not in us but in God. Therefore, "my" life isn't "my" anything. Justin Holcomb says:

> Before any discussion of what we should *do*, we must understand deeply in our bones who we *are*: the workmanship of God. You are his project. So, you are invited to be who you are. Your life is not your own; it was bought with a price. Live with the gratitude, humility, joy and peace that come from knowing it does not all depend on you. You are loved and accepted in Christ, so you don't have to focus on what you do or don't do for God. Now you can focus on what Jesus has done for you, and that will cause you to love God more. Then you can't help but walk in grace, realizing how costly God's grace was.[422]

Jesus is the ultimate expression of love, and it is He who personifies "grace upon grace."[423] To understand the Bible or the gospel at all, one must first come to the realization that had it not been for the grace of God, nothing would be possible. He continues to act faithfully toward us in spite of the fact that we act faithless toward Him.

What Christians should know is that grace is the one-way street from God to us that makes everything possible.

---

[420] Augustine, *Against the Letters of the Pelagians*, I.iii.6
[421] Ephesians 2:8-10
[422] Justin S. Holcomb, *On the Grace of God* (Wheaton, IL: Crossway, 2013), 94
[423] John 1:16

II. Stewardship

One of the most natural extensions of a discussion about grace is a discussion of stewardship. What Christians should know is that a *steward* is someone who has the responsibility of managing and looking after someone else's things.

A person therefore becomes a steward and has an identity solely as a function of the real owner. A steward owns nothing and has no rights to the assets that he or she is managing. One of the earliest examples of stewardship occurs in Genesis 2:15-17 where the text says, "Then the LORD God took the man and put him into the Garden of Eden to cultivate it and keep it. The LORD God commanded the man, saying, 'From any tree of the garden you may eat freely; but from the tree of the knowledge of good and evil you shall not eat, for in the day that you eat from it you will surely die.'"

Because Adam is part of the creation, he received everything he had (e.g., free food, the command to take dominion and to "be fruitful and multiply,"[424] life in the Garden of Eden, and a wife[425]) exclusively *because* of the Creator, God. In fact, in order to fulfill God's first command to humankind to "be fruitful and multiply" people *had to look* away from themselves and toward someone else. In Hebrew, the root of the world fruitful, *para*, means to bear fruit. Therefore, in order to be fruitful, the fruit *cannot be consumed* and the seeds must be planted—this necessitates not only future-preference, but also other-preference.

In the same light, looking back to Genesis 2:15-17, the roots of the words cultivate and keep are *abad* and *samar*, respectively. *Abad* by implication means to serve, be a husbandman, or to worship. *Samar* means to hedge about as it pertains to thorns, or to keep, protect, guard, preserve, and to be a watchman. God didn't require a cultivator or a keeper to be on His payroll, but stewardship was granted nonetheless. A very powerful lesson to be drawn from these few verses is that we are given many gardens (i.e., institutions that have the potential to bring about

---

[424] Genesis 1:28
[425] Genesis 2:21-23

new life and multiply, such as marriage, jobs, parenting, a calling, and the church) in our lives that require upkeep and maintenance. A proper steward does not adopt the attitude of an hourly employee who waits to clock out when the shift is over. Instead, a steward realizes that many things in the garden require constant maintenance and care, and proper preservation will yield a garden spilling over with life. To "be fruitful and multiply" means the future potential always exceeds the present limitation(s), but in order to achieve that future requires work. This stewardship is a form of worship (*abad*) in recognition of and honoring the LORD. As any gardener will tell you, cultivating a thriving garden requires diligence, focus, and a persistent dedication to hedge against the thorns (*samar*).

Everything in our existence belongs to God.[426] In fact, without God, human beings are simply *apar*, or a heap of ashen rubbish.[427] Everything that we are and everything that we do is therefore a function of Him alone. This is why in John 3:27, John the Baptizer says, "A man can receive nothing unless it has been given him from heaven."

In a Biblical sense, the Greek word for steward is *oikonomos*, a superintendant (or an overseer) who is entrusted to manage the affairs of a household who is also responsible for dealing out the proper portion to every other servant in the house *and* to the children who are not yet self-sufficient. Hence, Biblical stewardship points away from self-gain and points directly to God, who gives away freely. Stewardship is not selfish; it is very generous. I Peter 4:10 says, "As each one has received a special gift, *employ it in serving one another as good stewards* of the manifold grace of God" (italics mine).

A classic example of stewardship can be seen in Ephesians 4, where the apostle Paul talks about the use of the gifts of the Spirit. It becomes very clear, then, that stewardship has very much to do with how we engage with others, and what our goals should always be. Ephesians 4:1-16 (NIV) says:

---

[426] I Chronicles 29: 12, 14; Psalm 24:1
[427] Genesis 2:7

> As a prisoner for the Lord, then, I urge you to live a life worthy of the calling you have received. Be completely humble and gentle; be patient, bearing with one another in love. Make every effort to keep the unity of the Spirit through the bond of peace ... But to each one of us grace has been given as Christ apportioned it ... So Christ himself gave the apostles, the prophets, the evangelists, the pastors and teachers, *to equip his people for works of service, so that the body of Christ may be built up until we all reach unity in the faith and in the knowledge of the Son of God and become mature*, attaining to the whole measure of the fullness of Christ. Then we will no longer be infants, tossed back and forth by the waves, and blown here and there by every wind of teaching and by the cunning and craftiness of people in their deceitful scheming. Instead, speaking the truth in love, we will grow to become in every respect the mature body of him who is the head, that is, Christ. From him the whole body, joined and held together by every supporting ligament, grows and builds itself up in love, as each part does its work (italics mine).

Paul is very clear for what purpose Christ gave the gift of grace to prophets, evangelists, pastors, and teachers: to equip others for works of service in order to built up the body of Christ. So, even the gifts that God bestows on some are never to be used for self-gain or self-promotion. Instead, those gifted with a special calling by God are always supposed to use those talents to build up a community of people who are nurtured on sound doctrine, will speak the truth, and do not waver by the deceitful treachery of the world.

Additionally, a discussion about stewardship involves a discussion about money, and roughly speaking, Jesus spoke about money 25 percent of the time in the New Testament.

II Corinthians 9:6-7 points to the fact that we must give with joy, knowing that God gives openly and abundantly out of love: "Now this I say, he who sows sparingly will also reap sparingly, and he who sows bountifully will also reap bountifully. Each one must do just as he has purposed in his heart, not grudgingly or under compulsion, for God loves a cheerful giver." Stewards strive to work harder to honor God and not for the praise of others,[428] and they remain righteous and faithful in their wealth and therefore are entrusted with "true riches."[429] They are not abusive,[430] conceited, angry, or selfish.[431] Good stewards also look at all the stuff that's been given to them and then ask, "How can I bless others with all this stuff?"[432] Stewardship is about contentment[433] not endless want, desire, or consumption.[434] Stewardship certainly does not covet;[435] stewards are trustworthy[436] and never allow the focus on self to overtake the focus on God.[437] Stewardship is very generous and self-sacrificial, because we are to follow Jesus's command and treat others with love.[438] II Corinthians 8:1-15 says:

> Now, brethren, we wish to make known to you the grace of God which has been given in the churches of Macedonia, that in a great ordeal of affliction their abundance of joy and their deep poverty overflowed in the wealth of their liberality. For I testify that according to their ability, *and beyond their ability*, they gave of their own accord, begging us with much urging for the favor of participation in the support of the saints, and this, not as we had expected, *but they first gave themselves to the Lord and to us by the will of God* ... For you know the grace of our Lord Jesus Christ, that though He was rich, *yet for your sake He became poor,* so that you through His poverty might be-

---

[428] Proverbs 16:3; Colossians 3:23. Also note that the Proverbs were written by Solomon, the richest man to have ever lived as noted in I Kings 3:13 and II Chronicles 9:22.
[429] Luke 16:11
[430] Luke 12:42-46
[431] Titus 1:7-10
[432] Proverbs 13:22; Acts 2:44-45.
[433] I Timothy 6:7-8
[434] Exodus 16:18; Proverbs 21:20
[435] Exodus 20:17
[436] I Corinthians 4:1-2
[437] Haggai 1:1-11
[438] John 15:12-14

come rich ... For if the readiness is present, it is acceptable according to what a person has, not according to what he does not have. For this is not for the ease of others and for your affliction, but by way of equality—at this present time *your abundance being a supply for their need, so that their abundance also may become a supply for your need, that there may be equality;* as it is written, "He who gathered much did not have too much, and he who gathered little had no lack" (italics mine).

In this model from the New Testament, it becomes very clear that those in the Macedonian churches gave freely and abundantly to their own detriment, and that their giving supplied the needs of those without so that individual success at the expense of others was not desired as something to be grasped. The Greek work *isotes* (*equality*, verse 14) means likeness in condition or proportion, fairness, or what is equitable.

Many modern economic systems encourage consumption, hoarding, and self-reliance, while the Biblical paradigm encourages sharing, giving, and mutual assistance. Our world is not detestable, but *the pattern* of the world is, and a less than admirable character governs our world.[439] Romans 12:2 says, "Do not conform to the *pattern* of this world" (italics mine; NIV). This is not an economic commentary, but any society built upon a pattern where "greed is good," "the market decides winners and losers," and success is defined by "how much purchasing power you have" clearly runs counter to the Biblical formulation of stewardship. Stewardship is the opposite of economic self-promotion, which is exactly why Christ said, "No one can serve two masters; for either he will hate the one and love the other, or he will be devoted to the one and despise the other. You cannot serve God and wealth."[440] Jesus also said in Matthew 13:22 that "the seed falling among the thorns refers to someone who hears the word, but the worries of this life and the deceitfulness of

---

[439] John 12:31; II Corinthians 4:4
[440] Matthew 6:24. See also Matthew 21:12 and John 2:15.

wealth choke the word, making it unfruitful" (NIV). Here, wealth is not labeled inherently bad, but it does carry with it a deceitfulness that cuts off the air that the Word needs to breathe in our lives.

What Christians should know is that the prosperity gospel is a fraud.

What Christians should know is that Christ did not die so that you could be rich.

What Christians should know is that if you love money and the world, then you serve a master that is not Jesus Christ.[441]

I Timothy 6:9-10 is the anti-prosperity gospel verse: "But those who want to get rich fall into temptation and a snare and many foolish and harmful desires which plunge men into ruin and destruction. For the love of money is a root of all sorts of evil, and some by longing for it have wandered away from faith and pierced themselves with many griefs."

This is not an attack on the wealthy. It is not an attack on success. I Timothy 6:9-10 speaks to those *who want to get rich*, not to affluence itself. I Timothy 6:17-19 does speak to those who are already rich: "Instruct those who are rich in this present world not to be conceited or to fix their hope on the uncertainty of riches, but on God, who richly supplies us with all things to enjoy. *Instruct them to do good, to be rich in good works, to be generous and ready to share*, storing up for themselves the treasure of a good foundation for the future, so that they may take hold of that which is life indeed" (emphasis added). It follows then that the wealthy are actually in a position to do more good works as a function of their blessings. This is therefore not a group to condemn, but a group to encourage.

Hence, the above verses are a polemic on the pursuit of money *as an end itself* or *the love of money*, which is the root of "all sorts of evil."[442] God isn't concerned so much with *if* you have money. He is concerned with how you use it. He does not tolerate the abuse of power or the oppression of others to secure

---

[441] Matthew 6:24
[442] I Timothy 6:10

financial gain.[443] God has made it very clear throughout the course of the Bible that He is in favor of blessing His servants, which is demonstrated in the lives of Abraham,[444] Isaac,[445] Joseph,[446] David,[447] Solomon,[448] and Job.[449] God blessed Solomon so much that he possessed riches greater than all of the kings both before and after him.[450] When God does give financial blessings, He makes it very clear *why* He does it: "He who steals must steal no longer; but rather he must labor, performing with his own hands what is good *so that he will have something to share with one who has need*" (italics mine).[451]

In the parable of the talents in Matthew 25:14-30, Jesus tells the story of a master who goes on a journey and entrusts his servants with different amounts of talents (money). When the master returns, he rewards the servants who received the most *because they made the most of their gift*. In fact, the text says the servant who received the most number of talents "immediately" went into action[452] upon receiving the gift. The servant who is subsequently called "wicked and lazy"[453] did nothing with his gift and buried his talent in the ground for "safekeeping."[454] Jesus advises everyone not to store up temporal treasures on earth but eternal treasures in heaven.[455] Christ was fully aware that where our money goes is where our heart goes. Ultimately, it is always better to give than to receive.[456]

Think of God as a very wealthy investor. He has many resources and isn't opposed to investing in different ventures, but

---

[443] Micah 2:1-2; James 5:1-6
[444] Genesis 13:2
[445] Genesis 26:12-14
[446] Genesis 39:2
[447] I Chronicles 29:28
[448] II Chronicles 9:20-22. Notably, Solomon had so much gold that silver lost value during his kingship.
[449] Job 1:1-3
[450] II Chronicles 1:11-12
[451] Ephesians 4:28
[452] Matthew 25:16
[453] Matthew 25:26
[454] Matthew 25:25
[455] Matthew 6:19-21
[456] Acts 20:35

as a smart investor, He seeks a return on His investment. If He blesses you with a little bit of money, and you blow it all on fruitless nonsense, why would He give you more? Yet, if He knows every time He invests talents in you, you quickly turn that initial sum into an even greater sum, He'll actually want to keep on investing because you have proven to be a worthwhile investment.

And here's the very interesting part about stewardship. God does not count how much you give. He counts *what you have left* as the barometer for how much you give. This is why in Matthew 12:41-44 it says, "And [Jesus] sat down opposite the treasury, and began observing how the people were putting money into the treasury; and many rich people were putting in large sums. A poor widow came and put in two small copper coins, which amount to a cent. Calling His disciples to Him, He said to them, "Truly I say to you, *this poor widow put in more than all the contributors to the treasury; for they all put in out of their surplus, but she, out of her poverty, put in all she owned*, all she had to live on" (italics mine).

Stewardship is *qualitative*—that is, it describes how you ought to use money and time, approach relationships, and behave in your vocation, just to give a few examples. The simplest way stewardship is *quantified* is tithing. The tithe[457] is a Biblical principle defined as the giving of the "first fruits,"[458] or the first ten percent,[459] of *gross earnings* to the LORD. Of course, God doesn't need money, but the gesture is a means to honor God and to show reverence for the One who gave you the money in the first place. When we think about stewardship and tithing, then, we ought not to think that we are giving God our first 10 percent. Instead, God is letting us keep 90 percent of what's His—a fantastic deal any way you look at it. The apostle Paul

---

[457] Exodus 25:2; Leviticus 27:30-33; Numbers 18:21, 26-28; Deuteronomy 14:22-26; Malachi 3:10
[458] Genesis 4:3-4; Exodus 23:19, 34:26; Leviticus 23:10-14; Numbers 18:13; Deuteronomy 26:2-4; II Chronicles 31:5; Nehemiah 10:35; Proverbs 3:9-10; Ezekiel 44:30; Romans 11:16
[459] Genesis 28:20-22; Leviticus 27:32; Hebrews 7:1-2

refers to giving as a form of sacrifice,[460] and thus a means of worship of God. Furthermore, God isn't waiting in Heaven for us to give our money only to spite us. He wants to bless us. Malachi 3:10 says, "'Bring the whole tithe into the storehouse, so that there may be food in My house, and test Me now in this,' says the LORD of hosts, 'if I will not open for you the windows of Heaven and pour out for you a blessing until it overflows.'" God rarely ever says, "test Me," but He invites people to give the tithe so that He may bless them abundantly. To deny God a tithe or to deny God the full tithe equates to robbing the LORD,[461] and disastrous consequences will result. Of course it goes without saying that if you truly have nothing, then it would be quite impossible to tithe. Hence, in II Corinthians 8:12 it says, "For if the willingness is there, the gift is acceptable according to what one has, not according to what one does not have."

It's worth mentioning that in the Old Testament, tithing had a very specific numerical value. In the New Testament, we see both in II Corinthians 8:1-15 and Matthew 12:41-44 that people were giving *beyond* ten percent. In the case of the members of the Macedonian churches, it says, "they gave according to their ability, and beyond their ability." In the poor widow's case, she gave everything that she had. In both cases, those who tithed had to make lifestyle adjustments in order to accommodate their tithing. For some of us, if we perceive 10 percent as a minimum from which we can then go above and beyond, this would coincide with the descriptions (not prescriptions) of certain instances of tithing in the New Testament.

To elaborate on robbing the LORD, consider Haggai 1:3-6, where God speaks about the depravity of His house (the Temple) while the people's houses are well furnished: "Then the word of the LORD came by Haggai the prophet, saying, 'Is it time for you yourselves to dwell in your paneled houses while this house lies desolate?' Now therefore, thus says the LORD of hosts, 'Consider your ways! You have sown much, but harvest little; you eat, but

---

[460] Philippians 4:18
[461] Malachi 3:8-9

there is not enough to be satisfied; you drink, but there is not enough to become drunk; you put on clothing, but no one is warm enough; and he who earns, earns wages to put into a purse with holes.'" If anyone has ever not fully tithed and felt as if they're putting wages "into a purse with holes," then you should pay very close attention to this story.

One of the reasons discussing tithing is so important is because in 21st century America, stewardship faces an uphill battle when it comes to money. The sad reality is that an overwhelming majority of Christians are *not* faithful economic stewards. This is evidenced by the fact that in 2012, research by the Barna Group revealed that "5% of adults qualify as having tithed—giving 10% or more of their annual income to a church or non-profit organizations." That means if you put 20 adults in a room, only 1 person gives the proper tithe. Keeping one's eyes on money keeps the gaze away from God. A house of faith built on a foundation of consumption simply will not stand. There is no inherent evil in money, but it has become very easy for the contemporary American to make wealth an all-powerful idol. But you don't have to take my word for it. Consider the wealthiest man in Biblical history, Solomon, and what he writes about the folly of riches in Ecclesiastes 5:10-16:

> He who loves money will not be satisfied with money, nor he who loves abundance with its income. This too is vanity. When good things increase, those who consume them increase. So what is the advantage to their owners except to look on? The sleep of the working man is pleasant, whether he eats little or much; but the full stomach of the rich man does not allow him to sleep. There is a grievous evil which I have seen under the sun: riches being hoarded by their owner to his hurt. When those riches were lost through a bad investment and he had fathered a son, then there was nothing to support him. As he had come naked from his mother's womb, so will he return as he came. He will take nothing from the fruit of his labor that he can carry in his hand. This also is a grievous evil— exactly as a man is born, thus will he die. So what is the advantage to him who toils for the wind?

The Hebrew word for vanity is *hebel*, a term used repeatedly in the book of Ecclesiastes. It means "emptiness, breath or vapor." Riches offer no true life—only a formless void. Only Jesus is the one who gives life, and when He blesses you with wealth, He intends for you to bless others with it. God incarnate left heaven, emptied Himself for the sake of humankind, and then left this world with nothing. That's a timeless example that we should all follow.

For Further Reading

Justin S. Holcomb, *On the Grace of God* (Wheaton, IL: Crossway, 2013).

CHAPTER VIII
THE CHURCH

Here are some questions that many churchgoers do not often consider: what is the Biblical definition of the church, and what function does it serve? Why should anyone go to church, and what are you expected to do in a church? From prior lessons, it is now clear that the five core principles of Christianity do not include a "church" of any kind, so where does one locate the church in the Christian walk?

As I shall explain, the church is much more than a "building" or an "institution." It serves to nurture, cultivate, and develop existing believers as well as to evangelize unbelievers. It is also a place where people can assemble in order to praise and worship God, participate in baptism and communion, and fellowship with others. The church is not responsible for salvation, does not atone for sins, and does not mediate between us and the Father—only Jesus does those things. The church therefore has no monopoly on God, nor does it have any ultimate power over your eternal life. Certainly, going to church and being an active church member *does not* make anyone righteous; only the LORD knows who are His,[462] and it is therefore futile for any of us to decide otherwise. Although the word "church" is used loosely in modern society, the Bible offers very specific prescriptions for what the church is and what it ought to do.

The church unifies and brings people together. As Ephesians 2:14 says, in Christ, "you who were formerly far off have been brought near by the blood of Christ. For He Himself is our peace, who made both groups into one and broke down the barriers of the dividing wall." As we shall discuss, members of the church, or

---

[462] II Timothy 2:19

the body of Christ, can be distinct, but they are not separate because all are joined together under the common banner of Jesus. Distinction *does not equal* separation.

Finally, one thing to keep in mind when studying the nature and functions of the church is to pay very close attention to the Holy Spirit, Who plays a "leading role" in the life of the church. Jesus, Who is the head of the church,[463] was conceived by the Holy Spirit,[464] and the Spirit anointed Jesus at His baptism.[465] Additionally, at the start of Jesus's public ministry, He read a scroll from Isaiah that read, "*The Spirit* of the LORD is upon Me, because *He anointed Me* to preach the gospel to the poor. He has sent me proclaim release to the captives, and recovery of sight to the blind, to set free those who are oppressed, to proclaim the favorable year of the LORD"[466] (italics mine). Hence, a church that is Spirit-filled and Spirit-led entails being like Jesus, Who was anointed, equipped, and empowered to do His earthly ministry by the Holy Spirit. The entire point of the church, then, is to continue the ministry of Jesus as God instructed His disciples in the Great Commission: "Go therefore and makes disciples of all nations, baptizing them in the name of the Father, Son, and the Holy Spirit".[467] God sent Jesus,[468] and now Jesus sends us.[469]

I. What is the Church?

What Christians should know is that the church is the faithful community of all those who are saved through belief in Jesus Christ as their Lord and Savior. Jesus is the head of the church.[470]

The "church" begins in Acts chapter 2 when the Holy Spirit descends from heaven on the Day of Pentecost. There, we learn

---
[463] Colossians 1:18
[464] Luke 1:34-35
[465] Luke 3:21-22
[466] Luke 4:18-19
[467] Matthew 28:19
[468] Luke 4:43; John 8:42
[469] John 17:18, 20:21
[470] Ephesians 1:22-23; 4:15-16; Colossians 2:19

that many were "together in one place" (v. 1) when the Holy Spirit filled the people, who then began speaking in foreign tongues. Subsequently, "devout men from every nation" came together (vv. 5-6) and were amazed because they heard the gospel in their own language. This unified the people for a common good under a common banner and reversed the division and separation that happened at the Tower of Babel.[471] This event coincides with the Biblical narrative that when God saves people, He brings them together, and when He judges, He separates them.

Next, the apostle Peter preaches a sermon and testifies to the saving power of Jesus, and the result was that "when they heard this, they were pierced to the heart, and said to Peter and the rest of the apostles, 'Brethren, what shall we do?' Peter said to them, 'Repent, and each of you be baptized in the name of Jesus Christ for the forgiveness of your sins; and you will receive the gift of the Holy Spirit'" (vv. 37-38). Those who received the gospel and were baptized began "continually devoting themselves the apostles' teaching and to fellowship, to the breaking of bread and to prayer ... all those who had believed were together and had all things in common ... day by day continuing with one mind ... praising God and having favor with all the people ... and the LORD was adding to their number day by day" (vv. 42-47).

So, what is the church? The short answer is found in Acts 2—the Holy Spirit empowering people and turning people's hearts and minds toward Jesus. This is a paradigm that transcends traditions and institutions and is a totally free and voluntary act open to any and all those who will hear and receive the good news.

The Greek word for church is *ekklesia*[472] meaning a religious congregation or an assembly of members on earth or of saints in heaven or both. Accordingly, the church is not one physical structure fixed in time, but a timeless institution that transcends

---

[471] Genesis 11
[472] For example, as used in Acts 20:28 and I Timothy 3:15.

any physical location. The church is both a tangible and a figurative organization. It is for the church that Christ gave up His life: "Christ also loved the church and gave Himself up for her."[473] The word church did not become familiar in the Bible until the writing of the New Testament, but the Old Testament offers several examples of God calling together a faithful community of those who believed in Him. In Acts 7:38, for example, the martyr Stephen uses the word *ekklesia* to refer to the Israelites who wandered in the wilderness. In fact, the Greek translation of the Old Testament (the Septuagint) uses the word *ekklesia* most frequently in order to translate the Hebrew word, *qahal*, which means "assembly" or "to gather."[474,475]

The church is the body of Christ that is ruled by Jesus. That authority to rule was granted by God: "And He put all things in subjection under [Jesus's] feet, and gave Him as head over all things to the church, which is His body, the fullness of Him who fills all in all."[476] Jesus exclusively builds the church (He calls it "My" church),[477] and in that building process, the LORD is the one Who adds people to churches.[478] The church equates to unity,[479] being made anew,[480] and fellowship among the members of the household of God.[481]

The church is both visible and invisible. A very easy way to think about this is that we can only see the visible church, whereas God is able to see both. The *ekklesia* that I can see includes my local church and the people who attend it as well as all the other churches and people around the world that I can visit or see in pictures. The invisible church, however, includes all those saints in heaven who serve as a "cloud of witnesses."[482]

---

[473] Ephesians 5:25b
[474] Wayne Grudem, *Systematic Theology* (Grand Rapids: Zondervan, 1994), 854.
[475] Examples of use of the word *qahal* include Genesis 28:3, Exodus 16:3, Numbers 10:7, Deut 4:10, and II Chronicles 1:3.
[476] Ephesians 1:22-23
[477] Matthew 16:18
[478] Acts 2:47
[479] Ephesians 2:14
[480] Ephesians 2:15
[481] Ephesians 2:19
[482] Hebrews 12:1

As Hebrews 11:4-32 mentions specifically, many faithful believers of the past are now enrolled in heaven and worship in the "church."[483] By implication, the invisible church is in a very secure position and is immune to corruption. The visible church is actually in a very precarious situation, where many "savage wolves" prey on sheep,[484] and false prophets attempt to deceive many.[485]

The Bible doesn't give a number that defines how many people a church must have, nor does the Bible state where the church must operate. Romans 16:5 and I Corinthians 16:9 label a church as a gathering in someone's house. In other places, the church refers to the assembly of an entire city,[486] and Acts 9:31 refers to a church throughout "all Judea and Galilee and Samaria." The New Testament also refers to the church that exists throughout the entire world.[487] Hence, the church is local, regional, global, earthly, and otherworldly. A simpler way of saying this is that the church is local and universal, and the local church is an expression of the universal church.

II. The Nature of the Church

A Biblical understanding of the church's nature will prime your mind to understand what the church is supposed to do. The apostle Paul uses many metaphors to explain the nature of the church, and a popular label is the bride of Christ. In Ephesians 5:31-32, he refers to the relationship between a husband and wife as analogous to Christ and the church: "For this reason a man shall leave his father and mother and shall be joined to his wife, and the two shall become one flesh. This mystery is great; but I am speaking with reference to Christ and the church." II Corinthians 11:2 also uses similar language: "For I am jealous for you with a godly jealousy; for I betrothed you to one husband, so

---

[483] Hebrews 12:23
[484] Acts 20:29-30
[485] Matthew 7:15-16
[486] I Corinthians 1:2; II Corinthians 1:1; I Thessalonians 1:1
[487] I Corinthians 12:28; Ephesians 5:25

that to Christ I might present you as a pure virgin." Generally speaking, Paul refers to the members of the church as members of a family and encourages believers to treat each other with the love that family members have for one another. Using this lens, everyone cares for and looks out for one another, and each exercises a selfless, sacrificial, and persistent dedication for the growth of the others. In I Timothy 5:1-2 Paul says, "Do not sharply rebuke an older man, but rather appeal to him as a father, to the younger men as brothers, the older women as mothers, and the younger women as sisters, in all purity." The head of this church family is the Father,[488] Who cares for and looks after His children.[489] As His children, we are thus all joined together in the family of God.[490]

The New Testament uses many other metaphorical examples to describe the church, including an olive tree,[491] a harvest,[492] branches on a vine,[493] a new temple built upon the cornerstone of Christ,[494] a pillar and support of the truth,[495] and the body of Christ.[496] The generous use of Biblical metaphors points directly to the dynamic and broad range of ways to view the church and what our relationship to it ought to look like. (And the word relationship is intentional, because the church is very relational, not merely an impersonal, lifeless "institution.") For example, the church as the bride of Christ means that as members of a church, we ought to be faithful and committed and graciously submitted to the church that seeks to care for, protect, and love believers. Hence, church hopping becomes a sign of unfaithfulness to your "spouse," and instead of demanding churches meet our requirements, we ought to ask, "How can I better serve my spouse?" The church as a pillar and support of

---

[488] Matthew 6:9, Ephesians 3:14
[489] II Corinthians 6:18; Galatians 4:1-7
[490] Matthew 12:49-50; I John 3:14-18
[491] Romans 11:17-24
[492] Matthew 13:1-30; John 4:35
[493] John 15:5
[494] I Peter 2:5-6
[495] I Timothy 3:15
[496] I Corinthians 12:12-27

the truth means we must diligently work to weed out non-truths and heresy. The church as the body of Christ means we ought to seek out and strive for unity with the common goal of service to Jesus. The church as a temple means it is more than a physical building, but a place to worship the LORD and abide in His presence.

Of note, Jesus is the true vine that is the church,[497] He is the one Who plants churches,[498] grows churches,[499] leads churches (the "Chief Shepherd"),[500] is present in churches,[501] and shuts churches down.[502] Paul describes Christ as being the head of the church body,[503] and each member of the body (e.g., the ears and the eyes) serves different roles in order execute proper functioning of the unified whole. Therefore, singular people will do dissimilar things, but each function derives its value as a part of the whole. *Distinction* but not *separation*. An eye by itself without a brain to interpret the light signal simply will not work, just as in order for a head to work, you need a neck to support it. If a toe tries to be an ear or if a hand tries to be an elbow, the results will be disastrous.

A portrait of the different gifts given to different people in the body of Christ is stated in I Corinthians 12:

> Now there are varieties of gifts, but the same Spirit. And there are varieties of ministries, and the same Lord. There are varieties of effects, but the same God who works all things in all persons. But to each one is given the manifestation of the Spirit for the common good. For to one is given *the word of wisdom* through the Spirit, and to another the *word of knowledge* according to the same Spirit; to another *faith* by the same Spirit, and to another *gifts of healing* by the one Spirit, and to another the *effecting of*

---

[497] John 15:1
[498] Hebrews 3:1-4
[499] Matthew 16:18
[500] I Peter 5:4
[501] Matthew 28:20
[502] Revelation 2:1-5
[503] Ephesians 1:22-23, 4:15-16; Colossians 2:19

miracles, and to another *prophecy*, and to another the *distinguishing of spirits*, to another *various kinds of tongues*, and to another the *interpretation of tongues*. But one and the same Spirit works all these things, distributing to each one individually just as He wills.

For even as the body is one and yet has many members, and all the members of the body, though they are many, are one body, so also is Christ. For by one Spirit we were all baptized into one body, whether Jews or Greeks, whether slaves or free, and we were all made to drink of one Spirit.

For the body is not one member, but many. If the foot says, "Because I am not a hand, I am not a part of the body," it is not for this reason any the less a part of the body. And if the ear says, "Because I am not an eye, I am not a part of the body," it is not for this reason any the less a part of the body. If the whole body were an eye, where would the hearing be? If the whole were hearing, where would the sense of smell be? But now God has placed the members, each one of them, in the body, just as He desired. If they were all one member, where would the body be? But now there are many members, but one body. And the eye cannot say to the hand, "I have no need of you"; or again the head to the feet, "I have no need of you." On the contrary, it is much truer that the members of the body which seem to be weaker are necessary; and those members of the body which we deem less honorable, on these we bestow more abundant honor, and our less presentable members become much more presentable, whereas our more presentable members have no need of it. But God has so composed the body, giving more abundant honor to that member which lacked, so that there may be no division in the body, but that the members may have the same care for one another. And if one member suffers, all the members suffer with it; if one member is honored, all the members rejoice with it.

> Now you are Christ's body, and individually members of it. And God has appointed in the church, first apostles, *second prophets, third teachers, then miracles, then gifts of healings, helps, administrations, various kinds of tongues.* All are not apostles, are they? All are not prophets, are they? All are not teachers, are they? All are not workers of miracles, are they? All do not have gifts of healings, do they? All do not speak with tongues, do they? All do not interpret, do they? But earnestly desire the greater gifts.
>
> And I show you a still more excellent way (all italics mine).

In the Scripture above, I italicized several of the specific gifts given by the Spirit as well as the different job titles that people will have in the service in the body of Christ. As the text says, everything is always done "for the common good," which means a gift given by God is to be used *in* the church and *for* the church. It is never meant for self-gain, self-promotion, or entrepreneurial endeavors. It is always meant to help other people and direct them toward Jesus.

III. What is the Church supposed to do?

Knowing what a church is supposed to do is important, because in the 21st century, many "churches" exist that do things antithetical to what the Bible teaches. You could have a dozen tree worshippers that form a "church," or a band of rebellious people who form a "church" based on false doctrine. So how does a Christian know what a Biblical church looks like?

One of the most succinct passages that describes what the body of Christ must do is found in Ephesians 4:1-16 (NIV). Essentially, this passage describes the unity and maturity in the body of Christ:

> As a prisoner for the Lord, then, I urge you to live a life worthy of the calling you have received. Be completely humble and gentle; be patient, bearing with one another in love. Make every effort to keep the unity of the Spirit through the bond of peace. There is one body and one

Spirit, just as you were called to one hope when you were called; one Lord, one faith, one baptism; one God and Father of all, who is over all and through all and in all ... So Christ himself gave the apostles, the prophets, the evangelists, the pastors and teachers, *to equip his people for works of service, so that the body of Christ may be built up until we all reach unity in the faith and in the knowledge of the Son of God and become mature, attaining to the whole measure of the fullness of Christ.* Then we will no longer be infants, tossed back and forth by the waves, and blown here and there by every wind of teaching and by the cunning and craftiness of people in their deceitful scheming. Instead, speaking the truth in love, we will grow to become in every respect the mature body of him who is the head, that is, Christ. From him the whole body, joined and held together by every supporting ligament, grows and builds itself up in love, as each part does its work. (emphasis added)

In essence, many different people playing many different roles work to build up the body of Christ into strong, mature believers who are firm in their beliefs, resistant to false doctrine, and equipped to do good works. These relationships and dynamics are characterized by peace, unity, love, and the common focus on Jesus.

The first thing a church must do is teach sound <u>Christian doctrine</u>. (By implication, that doctrine should also be heard and received by others). John Calvin said that "wherever we see the Word of God purely preached and heard, and the sacraments administered according to Christ's institution, there, it is not to be doubted, a church of God exists."[504] In speaking to Titus, a leader in a church, the apostle Paul says, "speak the things which are fitting for sound doctrine".[505] In the same letter, Paul writes that one of the qualifications of a church leader is one who holds "fast the faithful word which is in accordance with the teaching,

---
[504] John Calvin, *Institutes* 4.1.9
[505] Titus 2:1

so that he will be able both to exhort in sound doctrine and to refute those who contradict".[506] II Timothy 4:2-4 says, "preach the word; be ready in season and out of season; reprove, rebuke, exhort, with great patience and instruction. For the time will come when they will not endure sound doctrine; but wanting to have their ears tickled, they will accumulate for themselves teachers in accordance to their own desires, and will turn away their ears from the truth and will turn aside to myths." II Timothy 3:16 says that, "All Scripture is inspired by God and profitable for teaching, for reproof, for correction, for training in righteousness." I Timothy 6:3-5 says, "If anyone advocates a different doctrine and does not agree with sound words, those of our Lord Jesus Christ, and with the doctrine conforming to godliness, he is conceited and understands nothing; but he has a morbid interest in controversial questions and disputes about words, out of which arise envy, strife, abusive language, evil suspicions, and constant friction between men of depraved mind and deprived of the truth, who suppose that godliness is a means of gain."

If sound doctrine is not taught and preached, essentially what you have is a "church" based upon a doctrine of human ideology or some other perversion that is not of God. Resultantly, although the label of "church" is applied, that assembly will be based on heresy and lead people astray. Paul openly criticized those churches that had major doctrinal problems, that deviated from the Word and whose moral principles were also lacking.[507] (It's no surprise that the two went hand in hand). The church at Corinth is a perfect example. Instead of following the Word, that church basically did what "felt good" and as a result, there were numerous divisions,[508] a reliance on worldly wisdom and reason (and therefore not on the Holy Spirit),[509] carnal behaviors,[510]

---

[506] Titus 1:9
[507] I Corinthians 3:1-4, 4:18-21, 5:1-2, 6; 6:1-8; II Corinthians 1:23-2:11, 12:20-13:10; Galatians 1:6-9, 3:1-5
[508] I Corinthians 1:10-12
[509] I Corinthians 2:1-9
[510] I Corinthians 3:3

susceptibility to false doctrines,[511] people engaging in communion in an unworthy manner,[512] drunkenness,[513] participation in pagan rituals,[514] sacrificing to demons,[515] and being led astray by idols.[516] The book of Revelation also speaks of "synagogues of Satan."[517] In contrast, Paul took great joy in the churches at Thessalonica and Philippi that were based upon strong doctrine and had upstanding characters.[518]

The second thing a church must do is administer the sacraments of baptism and communion. Baptism and communion will each be discussed in greater detail in the second volume of *What Christians Should Know*. Essentially, baptism is an outward sign of the inward change of a person's new life with Jesus. The baptism thus is the start of a relationship between the person and God, and communion is the outward sign and a symbol of the continuance of that relationship.

The third thing a church must do is "look up" and worship God. Paul tells the church at Colossae "Let the word of Christ richly dwell within you, with all wisdom teaching and admonishing one another with psalms and hymns and spiritual songs, singing with thankfulness in your hearts to God."[519] Paul also says in Ephesians 1:11-13, "Also we have obtained an inheritance, having been predestined according to His purpose who works all things after the counsel of His will, to the end that we who were the first to hope in Christ would be *to the praise* of His glory" (italics mine). He tells those at the church in Ephesus to make "the most of your time ... be filled with the Spirit, speaking to one another in psalms and hymns and spiritual songs, singing and making melody with your heart to the Lord."[520]

---

[511] II Corinthians 11:3-4
[512] I Corinthians 11:23-33
[513] I Corinthians 11:21
[514] I Corinthians 8
[515] I Corinthians 10:20
[516] I Corinthians 12:2
[517] Revelation 2:9, 3:9
[518] Philippians 1:3-11, 4:10-16; I Thessalonians 1:2-10, 3:6-10; II Thessalonians 1:3-4, 2:13
[519] Colossians 3:16
[520] Ephesians 5:16-19

The fourth thing a church must do is "look in" and nurture believers. Colossians 1:28 (NIV) says, "He is the one we proclaim, admonishing and teaching everyone with all wisdom, *so that we may present everyone fully mature in Christ*" (emphasis added). Ephesians 4:11-13 says, "So Christ himself gave the apostles, the prophets, the evangelists, the pastors and teachers, *to equip his people for works of service, so that the body of Christ may be built up until we all reach unity in the faith and in the knowledge of the Son of God and become mature*, attaining to the whole measure of the fullness of Christ" (italics mine). Many times in the New Testament, nurturing those in the church also involves material help.[521]

The fifth thing a church must do is "look out" and evangelize non-believers. In the great commission, Jesus told His disciples to "Go and make disciples of all nations, baptizing them in the name of the Father and of the Son and of the Holy Spirit, and teaching them to obey everything I have commanded you."[522] As Wayne Grudem says, "The evangelistic work of declaring the gospel is the primary ministry that the church has toward the world."[523] This evangelism includes proclaiming the gospel, being merciful to those who would rather not hear it,[524] and being kind and gracious to *all* people.[525]

The LORD Jesus, the head of the church, portrays evangelism in John 4 when He engages the Samaritan woman. In fact, this is the longest recorded conversation Jesus had with anyone in the entire New Testament, and it was with a non-believer (at least initially), a woman, and a Samaritan (Jewish men and Samaritan women were like oil and water back in those days). Jesus traveled far out of His way and became wearied[526] in His quest to find this woman, and when He did find her, He defied customary social boundaries to speak frankly to a woman living

---

[521] Acts 11:29; II Corinthians 8:4; I John 3:17
[522] Matthew 28:19
[523] Wayne Grudem, *Systematic Theology* (Grand Rapids: Zondervan, 1994), 868.
[524] Luke 6:35-36
[525] Luke 4:40
[526] John 4:6

in sin. Because His act defied expectations, and because He took the time to speak with a person who was deemed "unclean," look at the extraordinary results: "So the woman left her waterpot, and went into the city and said to the men, 'Come, see a man who told me all the things that I have done; this is not the Christ, is it?' They went out of the city, and were coming to Him ... From that city many of the Samaritans believed in Him because of the word of the woman who testified, 'He told me all the things that I have done.' So when the Samaritans came to Jesus, they were asking Him to stay with them; and He stayed there two days. Many more believed because of His word; and they were saying to the woman, 'It is no longer because of what you said that we believe, for we have heard for ourselves and know that this One is indeed the Savior of the world'".[527]

In analyzing the call to look up, in, and out, it is important to understand that the whole interprets the part and all angles of vision have to be treated equally. For example, a church that does not look up to God can cast their eyes on an idol, therefore "nurturing" their congregants with tainted milk leading to spiritual sickness. A lack of sound doctrine will lead to superficial believers who may then evangelize but not be able to effectively minister to others whose degree of scrutiny exceeds the comprehension of the missionary. And superficial believers will be very susceptible to changing tides, wavering between opinions, and shaking like reeds in the wind. Too much emphasis on looking in without looking out will raise up strong disciples, but those disciples will never get out of the building. Subsequently, speaking metaphorically about the body of Christ, it now becomes very clear that as a unified "church," some body parts will do much more of one thing (e.g., singers who lead worship, pastors who lead teaching, and missionaries who lead evangelism) and subsequently do very little of others because different parts have specialized functions.

The sixth thing a church must do is strive for unity and purity in the things that it does. Under the banners of "unity" and

---

[527] John 4:28-30, 39-42

"purity," the list of specific requirements that a church must execute is very long, but the point is that every member of a church has to be on the same general page, and the things that they do must be effective. So, it makes no sense if ABC church looks up, in, and out very well and routinely performs baptisms and communions, but the married pastor is sleeping with the choir director and the evangelists routinely get drunk in order to "fellowship" with non-believers. So, in pursuit of unity (i.e., "one flock and one shepherd")[528] and purity, the church also seeks to "[admonish] and [teach] everyone with all wisdom" so that believers may fully mature in Christ.[529]

Furthermore, the church must not only teach sound doctrine, but must also equip its members to refute false doctrine,[530] have *qualified* leadership,[531] silence teachers of false doctrine,[532] maintain the purity of the Christian faith,[533] execute the sacraments of baptism and communion *properly*,[534] execute church discipline to correct those who deviate from proper conduct,[535, 536] *effectively* worship,[537] *effectively* witness,[538] properly govern the church,[539] demonstrate spiritual power in the ministries of the church,[540] promote personal holiness,[541]

---

[528] John 10:16, 17:21, 23; I Corinthians 1:2, 10, 13, 10:17, 12:12-26; Ephesians 4:3; Philippians 2:2
[529] Colossians 1:28
[530] Titus 1:9
[531] I Timothy 2 and 3
[532] Titus 1:11
[533] Jude 3
[534] I Corinthians 11:17-34
[535] I Corinthians 5:6-7, 12-13
[536] Church discipline is always meant to restore, reconcile, and prevent sin from spreading to others. Discipline is executed just as a loving father disciplines his son (cf. Proverbs 13:24; Hebrews 12:6; Revelation 3:19). For the prevention on the spreading of sin, see I Corinthians 5:2, 6-7; Hebrews 12:15. Matthew 18:15-17 provides the blueprint for conflict resolution, and the following verses detail examples *for what* church discipline is to be exercised: heresy (II John 10-11), blasphemy (I Timothy 1:20), divisiveness (Romans 16:17; Titus 3:10), incest (I Corinthians 5:1), laziness (II Thessalonians 3:6-10), and disobedience (II Thessalonians 3:14-15).
[537] Ephesians 5:18-20; Colossians 3:16-17
[538] Matthew 28:19-20; John 13:34-35; Acts 2:44-47; I John 4:7
[539] I Timothy 3:1-13
[540] Acts 1:8; Romans 1:16; I Corinthians 4:20; II Corinthians 10:3-4; Galatians 3:3-5; II Timothy 3:5

care for those without,[542] build up the church,[543] and of course, love Jesus.[544] The unity of the church is something that is very valuable, because innumerable forces are at play that seek to divide and destroy the church.[545] Jude says there are rebellious people who actually set out to split up the church: "These are the ones who cause divisions, worldly-minded, devoid of the Spirit."[546]

Of course, all of these activities apply to the visible church and not the invisible church. And in the quest for church purity, it becomes very clear that *everything* centers around Jesus. A church that suggests an answer to a problem that is not Jesus or when Christ is not the head of the church, then what is supposed to be a house of faith has now turned into a house of manmade ideology where prescriptions are given for behavior change, personal improvement, or outlets for socialization that do not involve the LORD at all.

Conclusion

As I hope it is has now become clear, the Biblical formulation for "church" stands in stark contrast to what many in 21st century America have accepted as the formal definition. It goes without saying that no church will excel in all of its functions all the time, but modern churches have often confused what is distinguishing from what is central. That is, although a church may do something very well, while that is something to be noted, if that excellence happens at the expense of other functions that are central to the church, then the "church" has ceased to do what the Bible says it should. For example, if a church has a magnificent music ministry, then that is a wonderful thing. But if in its *distinction*, that church places its resources in music and

---

[541] I Thessalonians 4:3; Hebrews 12:14
[542] Acts 4:32-35; Romans 15:26; Galatians 2:10
[543] I Corinthians 14:12
[544] I Peter 1:8; Revelation 2:4
[545] Romans 16:17-18
[546] Jude 19

worship at the expense of sound doctrine and evangelism, then the church's *central* functions will suffer.

This also speaks directly to the modern fascination with church "marketing" that actually uses business techniques in order to "promote" the church to certain demographics and market segments by engineering programs and activities to "attract" certain cohorts. God is the only Person Who plants, builds, leads, runs, and adds members to a church. Resultantly, "planning" and "vision" become a function of what *we* can do in order to materialize a yet-to-be-determined future and recruit more "customers." In this dynamic, the congregants are being attracted to things that are appealing *to them*, so once those big flashing lights go away, attendance plummets. The focus shifts away from learning sound doctrine, praising God, and spreading the good news to others. Instead, the focus becomes a matter of personal fulfillment.

CHAPTER IX
REGENERATION

I have written much so far about central *principles* of the Christian faith—ideas that, to some, may feel far away or removed from their personal experience. This lesson on regeneration by far contains the most palpable *applications* to each person's existence because, in the end, one of the most central questions will be, "How will all of this change my life?" Regeneration thus helps believers answer the question, "How do I know I am saved?" Think of the prior lessons being like a business's overall motto—for example, "Finger lickin' good." That may sound great but provides no specific details or guidelines on how an employee's day will look in pursuit of "Finger lickin' good." Regeneration does just that—by providing a glimpse of the daily experience—in the walk of the Christian.

Specifically, regeneration means being born again by the Holy Spirit and being given a new heart and mind. Wayne Grudem defines regeneration as "a secret act of God in which he imparts new spiritual life to us; sometimes called 'being born again.'"[547] Regeneration is part of the entire process of salvation that continues Christ's atoning sacrifice in the cross—that is, Christ has paid the price for our sins, and the Holy Spirit actualizes that work in our lives so that He can put sin to death and raise us up to new life. Regeneration, or being "born again," is totally and completely dependent on God[548] in the same way that our natural births were not an active, voluntary choice on our part.

Certainly, there is a very specific ordering of salvation, called the *ordo salutis*, and each other component (election, calling,

---

[547] Wayne Grudem, *Systematic Theology* (Grand Rapids: Zondervan, 1994), 699.
[548] John 3:3-8; I Peter 1:3; cf. James 1:18

[regeneration], conversion, justification, adoption, sanctification and perseverance) will be discussed separately in a future volume of *What Christians Should Know*. Because salvation has a specific order, confusion about the sequence will result in divergent beliefs about how someone enters into and engages in a relationship with God. Regeneration is part of a sequence and sets the tone of a Christian's life after he or she has been elected and called. Furthermore, the Bible teaches us that in order to be regenerated, we had to be exposed to the Word of God and hear the gospel. James 1:18 says, "In the exercise of His will He brought us forth *by the word of truth*, so that we would be a kind of first fruits among His creatures" (italics mine). I Peter 1:23-25 says, "For you have been born again not of seed which is perishable but imperishable, that is, *through the living and enduring word of God*. For, 'All flesh is like grass, And all its glory like the flower of grass. The grass withers, And the flower falls off, But the word of the Lord endures forever.' And this is *the word which was preached to you*" (emphasis added).

Calling can therefore be thought of as God speaking to us *from the outside* and summoning us to Him; regeneration, then, is the Holy Spirit working on us *from the inside* so that we can respond faithfully to God and live a Christ-centered life. As Jesus said in John 6:44, "No one can come to Me unless the Father who sent Me draws him; and I will raise him up on the last day."[549] An example of this truth can be seen in Acts 10:44-48. Here, the apostle Peter preaches the good news to the house of Cornelius, *and then* all those who hear were overpowered by the Holy Spirit:

> While Peter was still speaking these words, the Holy Spirit fell upon all those who were listening to the message. All the circumcised believers who came with Peter were amazed, because the gift of the Holy Spirit had been poured out on the Gentiles also. For they were hearing them speaking with tongues and exalting God. Then Peter

---

[549] See also John 6:65.

answered, "Surely no one can refuse the water for these to be baptized who have received the Holy Spirit just as we did, can he?" And he ordered them to be baptized in the name of Jesus Christ.

Similarly, in Acts 16:13-14, the apostle Paul preaches the gospel to a crowd of women, and one of the women, Lydia, had her heart opened by the LORD. The text says, "and we sat down and began speaking to the women who had assembled. A woman named Lydia, from the city of Thyatira, a seller of purple fabrics, a worshiper of God, was listening; and the Lord opened her heart to respond to the things spoken by Paul." As Paul says in Romans 10:17, "Faith comes from hearing, and hearing by the word of Christ."

Regeneration is total, not partial: "Therefore if anyone is in Christ, he is a new creature; the old things passed away; behold, new things have come."[550] Before regeneration, we were dead in our whole being.[551] God thus aims to make us new creations in regeneration—not slightly used, or almost new—but brand new creations. The Greek word for new, *kainos*, implies freshness in respect to an unheard of or unprecedented novel *substance*. From this concept stems the conclusion that regeneration is a finite *event* in the Christian's life, yet the effects of that regeneration will manifest *over time*. Hence, God's work is always good, full, and complete while our response is gradual and a "work in progress." Of course, regeneration does not mean that a Christian will live a perfect life. Rather, it means that the life of a Christian will not be characterized by continued indulgence in sin.

I. By Grace Alone

We spoke about the grace of God previously. Specifically, regeneration is a special type of grace imparted on people who

---

[550] II Corinthians 5:17
[551] Ephesians 2:1

are otherwise totally undeserving.[552] This act of grace is performed by the Holy Spirit,[553] and without the grace of regeneration (i.e., without God), *no one could be saved* and therefore have eternal life.[554] This is why the idea of God's grace is so important. The Holy Spirit is the divine Helper[555] and Teacher[556] that not only gives us the power to become regenerated, but also to continually repent and turn toward God, set our minds on Christ, live according to the Spirit, and belong to Jesus.[557]

Accordingly, no one can "self-regenerate" and live a more Christ-centered life by his or her own initiative. Titus 3:5 says, "*He saved us*, not on the basis of deeds which we have done in righteousness, but according to His mercy, by the washing of regeneration and renewing by the Holy Spirit" (italics mine). In Matthew 19:28, Jesus said, "Truly I say to you, that you who have followed Me, in the regeneration when the Son of Man will sit on His glorious throne, you also shall sit upon twelve thrones, judging the twelve tribes of Israel." The gift of this special grace to undeserving sinners is alluded to in the New Covenant in Jeremiah 32:38-41, which says:

> They shall be My people, and I will be their God; and *I will give them one heart and one way*, that they may fear Me always, for their own good and for the good of their children after them. I will make an everlasting covenant with them that I will not turn away from them, to do them good; and *I will put the fear of Me in their hearts so that they will not turn away from Me*. I will rejoice over them to do them good and will faithfully plant them in this land with all My heart and with all My soul (emphasis added).

The word heart (*leb* in Hebrew, meaning the center of everything) is used frequently in the Old Testament, and it

---

[552] Ephesians 2:1-5
[553] John 3:5-8
[554] John 3:3, 5; cf. I Corinthians 2:6-16
[555] John 14:26, 16:7
[556] John 16:13
[557] Romans 8:4-13; Ephesians 5:18

symbolically denotes the essence of someone's being, their core identity and internal self. How we act;[558] how we think,[559] know[560] and understand;[561] and what we say[562] therefore stem from our heart condition. So, when the Old Testament speaks of the heart, it becomes clear how this is seen through the lens of regeneration and its profound internal work on our inner self. Deuteronomy 30:6 says, "Moreover the LORD your God will circumcise your heart and the heart of your descendants, to love the LORD your God with all your heart and with all your soul, so that you may live." Ezekiel 11:19-20 says, "And I will give them one heart, and put a new spirit within them. And I will take the heart of stone out of their flesh and give them a heart of flesh, that they may walk in My statutes and keep My ordinances and do them. Then they will be My people, and I shall be their God." Other examples of a regenerated heart in the Old Testament can be seen in Jeremiah 24:7, 31:31-33, and Ezekiel 36:26-27.

In the New Testament, regeneration is often referred to as being "born again." So, every human being is "born" in a natural sense as a general gift of grace from God. Only select people who have been elected[563] by God and hear the gospel call[564] receive the special gift of grace to be spiritually born again. I Peter 1:3 says, "Blessed be the God and Father of our Lord Jesus Christ, who according to His great mercy has caused us to be born again to a living hope through the resurrection of Jesus Christ from the dead." Mark Driscoll says:

> Regenerating grace is the source of all that it means to live as a Christian. As new creations with new hearts we have new passions, new desires, and new purposes, which culminate in a passionate life of joy and good works ... at its deepest level, the new heart longs for the

---

[558] Proverbs 4:4, 5:12, 10:8; Matthew 5:28, 6:21; Mark 7:21-23
[559] Proverbs 6:14, 25; 16:1
[560] Proverbs 2:10, 3:1-3, 23:15
[561] Proverbs 2:2, 24:32
[562] Matthew 12:34
[563] John 15:16; Ephesians 1:4-5; Romans 8:28-30
[564] Mark 16:15; Romans 10:14-17; I Corinthians 9:16; Revelation 3:20

desires of God and rejoices in the freedom that comes in replacing old sinful longings with new holy longings that give God glory and us joy.[565]

The clearest elucidation of being born again occurs in John 3, when Jesus speaks to Nicodemus. Christ explains that while we are all naturally alive, we are spiritually dead.[566] In order to become spiritually alive with Christ,[567] we must experience another birth—that of our spirit—and hence, be born again. John 3:3-8 (NIV) says:

> Jesus replied, "Very truly I tell you, no one can see the kingdom of God unless they are born again." "How can someone be born when they are old?" Nicodemus asked. "Surely they cannot enter a second time into their mother's womb to be born!" Jesus answered, "Very truly I tell you, no one can enter the kingdom of God unless they are born of water and the Spirit. Flesh gives birth to flesh, but the Spirit gives birth to spirit. You should not be surprised at my saying, 'You must be born again.' The wind blows wherever it pleases. You hear its sound, but you cannot tell where it comes from or where it is going. So it is with everyone born of the Spirit."

Again it is important to recognize that it is the work of the Holy Spirit that executes this rebirth. Being born again means that a person becomes a partaker of the divine nature[568] and is a new man[569] as well as a new creation where the old has passed away.[570] Someone who is born again is now the workmanship of Jesus, built to do good works.[571] (Many other passages of the New Testament speak about being born again.[572])

---

[565] Mark Driscoll, *Religion Saves* (Wheaton, IL: Crossway, 2009), 119.
[566] Ephesians 2:1, 5; Colossians 2:13
[567] Ephesians 2:5; Colossians 2:13
[568] II Peter 1:4
[569] Ephesians 2:15, 4:24
[570] II Corinthians 5:17
[571] Ephesians 2:10
[572] John 1:13; Romans 6:1-23; I Peter 1:3, 23

Hence, a person with a regenerated heart says, "I delight to do Your will, O my God; Your Law is within my heart."[573]

II. The Effects

What this means in a practical sense is that regenerated people will turn away from what *they* want to do and what *their* desires are and seek to honor, praise, and worship the LORD in *all* that they do. I John 3:9 says, "No one who is born of God practices sin, because His seed abides in him; and he cannot sin, because he is born of God." A prime example would be in regard to sexual immorality. An unrepentant, non-regenerated person would say, "I do what feels good." A regenerated, repentant person would "flee immorality"[574] because, as Paul says in I Corinthians 6:19-20, "Do you not know that your body is a temple of the Holy Spirit who is in you, whom you have from God, and that you are not your own? For you have been bought with a price: therefore glorify God in your body."

Regeneration, then, forces us to reconsider how we behave, because sin is an offense to God. When given the option to sleep with another man's wife, Joseph recognized that whatever he intended to do, at its core, the act was an offense to the LORD: "How then could I do this great evil and sin against God?"[575] David expresses similar sentiments in Psalm 139. He recognizes that nothing is hidden from God, and therefore he pursues God in all that he does: "Where can I go from Your Spirit? Or where can I flee from Your presence? If I ascend to heaven, You are there; If I make my bed in Sheol, behold, You are there ... Search me, O God, and know my heart; Try me and know my anxious thoughts; And see if there be any hurtful way in me, And lead me in the everlasting way."[576]

Regeneration recognizes that our lives are no longer our own: we are living *for* God. It is only by the power of the Holy

---
[573] Psalm 40:8
[574] I Corinthians 6:18
[575] Genesis 39:9
[576] Psalm 139:8-9, 23-24

Spirit that we can put away the old, deceitful ways of sin and put on the new self, created in righteousness and truth.[577] We put sin to death and consider the members of our earthly bodies dead to "immorality, impurity, passion, evil desire, and greed."[578] We put aside "anger, wrath, malice, slander, and abusive speech."[579] And we must never forget that these changes occur as a function of the Holy Spirit, not ourselves. This powerful realization frees us from any legalism or rule following that gives anyone a sense of earned righteousness or, even more dangerous, spiritual pride.

Regenerated people have a new God. If you worked in an office, you would have a boss. You would know your boss's personality, what he or she is like, and generally speaking, what he or she expects from you. If you switched to a different job, you would then have to learn a whole new set of guidelines for your new boss, who would undoubtedly be different. At this new work, you will adjust how you dress, how you speak, how you address others, and the overall way in which you carry yourself. With Jesus as our new Lord, God, and Savior, we no longer adhere to the old rules and expectations of our old "job." We are no longer slaves to sin, but we are free to obey God. We are no longer in bondage, but we are liberated in order to prepare ourselves to occupy (eventually) eternal life with God. At the core of every regenerated person's heart, they have an acute understanding that their boss is Yahweh, and they belong to Yahweh. From that heart condition grows an identity that says, "Yahweh is God, and I follow Him *alone*."

I John 5:18 says, "We know that no one who is born of God sins; but He who was born of God keeps him, and the evil one does not touch him." Hence, we are no longer loyal to our old ideology, bad habits, and way of thinking. And because we now serve the LORD and the LORD alone, every other functional "savior" is destroyed. So, if you worshipped marriage, the functional savior of a mate is no longer a top priority. If you

---

[577] Ephesians 4:17-24
[578] Colossians 3:5
[579] Colossians 3:8

worshipped wealth, the functional savior of money is now dead. If you worshipped approval, then the functional savior of affirmation is destroyed.

Regenerated people have a new identity (internal condition) and behave differently (external condition). II Corinthians 5:17 speaks of being a new creation. Godly creations, then, mirror God's characteristics such as holiness, truth, justice, and peace. But in order to begin *acting* like a new creation, one must first embrace the *internal change* in heart condition. If this were not the case, then we would *not* be saved by faith alone through grace alone but by works alone. Behavior proceeds out *from* a new identity. I John 2:29 says, "If you know that He is righteous, you know that everyone also who practices righteousness is born of Him." Being born again comes first, and then the practice of righteousness.

Regeneration is always God-dependant and human exclusive. This is what Paul referred to in Galatians 6:15, where he writes, "For neither is circumcision anything, nor uncircumcision, but a new creation." Circumcision is something we can do, *an act* that is an external sign. A new creation is something only God can do *on the inside*. In fact, regeneration causes such a change in people that often in the Bible, regenerated people are given a new name—for example, Abram is called Abraham, Jacob is called Israel, Cephas is called Peter, and Saul is called Paul.

Ephesians 4:22-23 says that we are renewed internally by laying "aside the old self, which is being corrupted in accordance with the lusts of deceit" and are "renewed in the spirit of [our minds]." Verse 24 says that that new self is in God's likeness. Our minds also change, and the new mindset is significantly different from the old mindset. I Corinthians 2:14-16 says:

But a natural man does not accept the things of the Spirit of God, for they are foolishness to him; and he cannot understand them, because they are spiritually appraised. But he who is spiritual appraises all things, yet he himself is appraised by no one. For who has known the mind of the Lord, that he will instruct Him? But we have the mind of Christ.

If you've ever wondered why, no matter how hard *you* try, some unbelievers just don't "get it," this verse should give you some clarity.

Regenerated people will no longer seek natural satisfaction, but rather, they seek the nourishing "spiritual milk"[580] that they will now crave in order to grow up and mature in Christ. And instead of rejecting the Word of God as burdensome and restrictive, they "joyfully concur with the law of God in the inner man."[581] They are more loving,[582] and they have new, Godly desires.[583] It's important to note exactly what Galatians 5:16-17 says: "But I say, walk by the Spirit, and you will not carry out the desire of the flesh. For the flesh sets its desire against the Spirit, and the Spirit against the flesh; for these are in opposition to one another, so that you may not do the things that you please." In other words, the Spirit does not condemn, riddle with guilt, or attempt to add legalism to desire in an absolute sense. The Spirit *desires* to do what is of God. The Greek word for desire is *epithymeo*, or "to set the heart upon, or to long for." Desire is morally neutral, but what makes *epithymeo* good or bad is *the target* of that desire (what one sets the desire upon). A life full of desire driven to do the things of God and empowered by the Holy Spirit is a very good thing indeed.

Of course, the temptation to sin always exists, and regenerated people will fall into sin. Regeneration does not make one sinless or immune to temptation. The difference between an

---

[580] I Peter 2:2
[581] Romans 7:22
[582] I John 4:7
[583] Psalms 37:4; Romans 7:4-6; Galatians 5:16-17

unbeliever, who is not regenerated, and a believer, who is regenerated, is that the latter is uncomfortable with his or her sin, seeks repentance, and does not desire to do what is offensive to God. A sinner can sin and sleep very comfortably. A believer can sin, but then things just won't feel right until he or she repents, asks for forgiveness, and runs back to God. This is why in Romans 7:15, Paul says, "For what I am doing, I do not understand; for I am not practicing what I would like to do, but I am doing the very thing I hate." A simple understanding of sin is that regenerated people change in their response to sin—they hate it, can't stand it, want to break free from it, and seek to destroy it.

Regenerated people also seek out other Christians with whom to fellowship as the church.[584] In essence, they seek out a new community, a new group of others to "hang out with" in God's family,[585] the body of Christ.[586] They also seek to worship God and to be in His presence.[587] They have new freedom[588] and new life, and that brand-new life looks, feels, and acts in a way that is very distinct from the old life. The new life bears the fruits of the Spirit since the Spirit regenerates us. A Spirit-filled and Spirit-led life turns away from, "immorality, impurity, sensuality, idolatry, sorcery, enmities, strife, jealousy, outbursts of anger, disputes, dissensions, factions, envying, drunkenness, carousing, and things like these" and instead is characterized by "love, joy, peace, patience, kindness, goodness, faithfulness, gentleness, [and] self-control."[589] I John 4:7 says, "Everyone who loves is born of God and knows God." Regeneration imparts in us the ability to say no to sin and yes to God: "For this is the love of God, that we keep His commandments; and His commandments are not burdensome. For whatever is born of God overcomes the world; and this is the victory that has overcome the world—our

---

[584] I John 1:3
[585] Ephesians 2:19-20
[586] Romans 12:5
[587] Ephesians 2:22
[588] Romans 6:6, 7:6
[589] Galatians 5:19-23

faith because greater is He who is in [us] than he who is in the world,"[590] and therefore we are sheltered and protected by attacks from the enemy who lures us away from God, for "He who was born of God keeps him, and the evil one does not touch him."[591]

Not everyone who says they believe in God, however, is in fact regenerated. Healthy trees produce good fruit, which is why Jesus warned in Matthew 7:15-20:

> Beware of the false prophets, who come to you in sheep's clothing, but inwardly are ravenous wolves. You will know them by their fruits. Grapes are not gathered from thorn bushes nor figs from thistles, are they? So every good tree bears good fruit, but the bad tree bears bad fruit. A good tree cannot produce bad fruit, nor can a bad tree produce good fruit. Every tree that does not bear good fruit is cut down and thrown into the fire. So then, you will know them by their fruits.[592]

In fact, we ought to never look for external signs as a barometer. Furthermore, *only God* knows who are His,[593] so trying to figure that out on our own is a futile endeavor. In Matthew 7:21-22, Jesus says, "Not everyone who says to Me, 'Lord, Lord,' will enter the kingdom of heaven, but he who does the will of My Father who is in heaven will enter. Many will say to Me on that day, 'Lord, Lord, did we not *prophesy* in Your name, and in Your name *cast out demons*, and in Your name *perform many miracles*?'" (italics mine). It is important to note that the double use of the word Lord is a term of endearment. What Jesus was trying to tell us is that we should all look up to God and pursue Him so that the Holy Spirit can regenerate us. Don't look out for signs and wonders, because that can very quickly get you into trouble.

Jesus said that John the Baptizer was the greatest human

---

[590] I John 4:4
[591] I John 5:18b
[592] cf. James 2:14-26.
[593] II Timothy 2:19

being to have ever lived.[594] Guess what John never did? Perform any miracles or exercise any demons. John the Baptizer, Paul, and Jesus never suggested that miracles or activities within the church should act as a barometer for "Christianness." These three each pointed to *character traits* in life as an indicator. Wayne Grudem says, "Genuine love for God and his people, heartfelt obedience to his commands, and the Christlike character traits that Paul calls the fruit of the Spirit, demonstrated consistently over a period of time in a person's life, simply *cannot* be produced by Satan or by the natural man or woman working in his or her own strength. These can only come about by the Spirit of God working within and giving us new life."[595]

What Christians should know is that regeneration focuses on the inward change of one's *heart condition*.

Our response to regeneration is a continual, day-by-day process. We will continue to be tempted to sin and will even fall into sin at times, but our response will be to repent and turn back toward God. Again, the apostle Paul clearly expresses this sentiment in Romans 7:15, where he writes, "For what I am doing, I do not understand; for I am not practicing what I would like to do, but I am doing the very thing I hate." Sin bothers regenerated people, and until they put sin to death, they will not be at peace.

The Bible prescribes that in order to be "filled" with the Holy Spirit[596] one ought to praise and worship God, address one another is psalms and hymns, and always give thanks to the LORD. The Greek word for "filled" is *pleroo* that not only implies one is to be so filled that nothing else is wanted, but the term is often used in nautical terms as it pertains to cramming a net or filling a sail with wind. Therefore, in order to get to where you want to go, you can't use one blast of wind. You need a constant, steady stream of wind while you navigate the waters of life in order to reach your destination. If you steer away from the direction the wind is blowing, you'll end up stranded at sea.

---

[594] Matthew 11:11; Luke 7:28
[595] Wayne Grudem, *Systematic Theology* (Grand Rapids: Zondervan, 1994), 706.
[596] Ephesians 5:18

CHAPTER X
WORSHIP

Worship is the topic of our last chapter because everything in the Christian's life should ultimately end at worship. Each and every thing that we do should be aimed at glorifying God. In this general sense, worship encompasses the totality of a person's thoughts and deeds. The Hebrew word for worship is *shacah*, which means to prostrate, to pay obeisance or to bow down in the presence of a superior. God is very clear that we ought never to worship anything other than Him. The Greek word for worship is *proskuneo*, which means to fawn or crouch to, to show reverence or to adore. By implication, these definitions clarify that worship is something that we do in the presence of God when we are both aware of Him and adore Him (thought), and, thus, we glorify Him (action) through singing and praising, for example.

The aforementioned action may also involve other people and our interactions with them. For example, Colossians 3:16 says, "Let the word of Christ richly dwell within you, with all wisdom teaching and admonishing one another with psalms and hymns and spiritual songs, singing with thankfulness in your hearts to God." *Only God* is worthy of worship, and this is why the first of the Ten Commandments is, "You shall have no other gods before Me" (Exodus 20:3). Exodus 34:14 says, "For you shall not worship any other god." Not even those beautiful, awesome and magnificent spiritual creations of God that serve Him are worthy of worship.[597] Only THE LORD is worthy to be praised and receive glory and honor because He and He alone created all things and is the first cause of everything. Revelation

---

[597] Revelation 22:8-9

4:11 says, "Worthy are You, our Lord and our God, to receive glory and honor and power; for You created all things, and because of Your will they existed, and were created." God will not give His glory to another,[598] and He is also a jealous God.[599] This jealousy should not conjure up ideas of a crazy lover or an overly emotional and irrational person; rather, it should make us keenly aware that when we divert worship away from the place where it truly belongs, this dishonors God and insults Him. God seeks His own honor because, as I hope I have made clear in the last nine chapters, everything He has done is not only worthy of that reverence, but it is also totally unmerited by us. On top of all of that, even though God is deserving of adoration, He never forces our hand. Instead, he invites us to voluntarily worship Him. And, in that voluntary worship, we are to use our gifts to always glorify[600] God and never glorify and bring attention to ourselves.

In the book of Isaiah, the prophet gives all human beings the meaning of life and specifically tells us why God made us: "Bring My sons from afar And My daughters from the ends of the earth, Everyone who is called by My name, *And whom I have created for My glory*, Whom I have formed, even whom I have made" (italics mine; 43:6-7). Ephesians 1:12 (NIV) says, "In order that we, who were the first to put our hope in Christ, might be *for the praise of his glory*" (emphasis added).

Glory is part of the worship formula because when you worship something, you also *glorify* it and *sacrifice* to it. The root of the word *glory* refers to honor, quantity, heaviness or something's physical weight. Hence, if you glorify something, you essentially put the "weight" and quantity of your thoughts, attention and resources into that thing—it's the thing you consider to be the most important. Sacrifice and glory go hand in hand because if you invest all your resources in something, you find yourself taking away from something else in order to glorify "it." We sacrifice *in order to* glorify. The ideal is to worship God

---

[598] Isaiah 48:11
[599] Exodus 20:5
[600] I Peter 4:11

and Him alone but, for example, people may worship their jobs and, consequently, put all their "weight," time and resources into their occupations. In so doing, they sacrifice their health, friends, and families to bring glory to "it." Romans 11:36-12:1 mentions the glory and sacrifice involved in worship: "For from Him and through Him and to Him are all things. To Him be the glory forever. Amen. Therefore I urge you, brethren, by the mercies of God, to present your bodies a living and holy sacrifice, acceptable to God, which is your spiritual service of worship."

The opposite of worshipping God is idolatry. Consequently, idolatry is worshipping anything that God created (e.g., nature, the planets, another person) or we made (e.g., an idea, a career, a lifestyle). Idolatry is an attempt to satisfy our own appetites with the objects of our choosing. That desire is never quenched because the appetite just comes back once our figurative stomachs are empty again. In Philippians 3:18-19, Paul says, "For many walk, of whom I often told you, and now tell you even weeping, that they are enemies of the cross of Christ, whose end is destruction, *whose god is their appetite*, and whose glory is in their shame, *who set their minds on earthly things*" (emphasis added). Romans 1:25 clarifies idolatry further: "They exchanged the truth of God for a lie, and worshiped and served the creature rather than the Creator, who is blessed forever." People may scoff, thinking that because they don't have little statues of "gods" in their houses, they can't have idols. However, idols are everywhere. The failure to recognize idols in 21st century America comes from the fact that many forms of idolatry are deemed socially acceptable. If you're curious about what your idols are, ask yourself a few simple questions:

(1) What Scriptures in the Bible do I disagree with? Why?

(2) What do I pray for or plan for the most?

(3) Where does my money go first?

(4) What do I center my life around?

(5) What is the one thing I need or want the most in my life right now?

God-centered worship is characteristic of people dedicated to THE LORD. He will take drastic measures to liberate those who have been prevented from worshipping Him. This is one reason why He freed Israel from Egyptian bondage. In Exodus 7:16 (NIV), God tells Pharaoh through Moses, "The LORD, the God of the Hebrews, has sent me to say to you: Let my people go, *so that they may worship me in the wilderness*" (italics mine). In many Biblical prophecies, we get a very clear picture that one of God's redemptive promises for all of humanity is their liberation from sin and the false idols of worship in the world so that they will be free to worship Him before His throne.[601]

Hebrews 12:22-29 depicts a heavenly scene where those who have accepted the gospel call and turned away from sin and false gods now praise and worship God as a communal body. Hence, heaven is a "church" worshipping and praising God:

> But you have come to Mount Zion and to the city of the living God, the heavenly Jerusalem, and to myriads of angels, to the general assembly and church of the firstborn who are enrolled in heaven, and to God, the Judge of all, and to the spirits of the righteous made perfect, and to Jesus, the mediator of a new covenant, and to the sprinkled blood, which speaks better than the blood of Abel.
>
> See to it that you do not refuse Him who is speaking. For if those did not escape when they refused him who warned them on earth, much less will we escape who turn away from Him who warns from heaven. And His voice shook the earth then, but now He has promised, saying, "YET ONCE MORE I WILL SHAKE NOT ONLY THE EARTH, BUT ALSO THE HEAVEN." This expression, "Yet once more," denotes the removing of those things which can be shaken, as of created things, so that those things which cannot be shaken may remain. Therefore, since we receive a kingdom which cannot be shaken, let us show gratitude, by which we may offer to God an acceptable service with reverence and awe; for our God is a consuming fire.

---

[601] For example, Isaiah 2:2-4, 25:6-8, 66:18-21; Jeremiah 49:6

Worship is never a forced activity that produces bitterness and grumbling. Rather, sincere worship changes the worshippers so that they delight in God. In fact, if you know any people who do not enjoy worship, then they are in for a surprise because heaven is a non-stop worship fest! [602] David, for example, wrote a large portion of the Psalms, passages intended to worship and praise God. In them, he says things such as, "One thing I have asked from the LORD, that I shall seek: / That I may dwell in the house of the LORD all the days of my life, / To behold the beauty of the LORD And to meditate in His temple" (27:4). He also writes, "In Your presence is fullness of joy; / In Your right hand there are pleasures forever" (16:11). In Psalm 73:25, Asaph writes, "Whom have I in heaven but You? / And besides You, I desire nothing on earth." In other cases, those engaged in genuine worship "[d]ay by day [continued] with one mind in the temple, and [broke] bread from house to house, they [took] their meals together with gladness and sincerity of heart, praising God and having favor with all the people" (Acts 2:46-47). Soon after Jesus's ascension, the disciples returned to Jerusalem and "were continually in the temple praising God."[603]

One of the most awe-inspiring verses in the Bible tells us that when we worship God, He, in turn, delights in us. In reference to the faithful in Zion who worship THE LORD, Isaiah 62:3-5 says:

> You will also be a crown of beauty in the hand of the LORD,
> And a royal diadem in the hand of your God.
> It will no longer be said to you, "Forsaken,"
> Nor to your land will it any longer be said, "Desolate";
> But you will be called, "My delight is in her,"
> And your land, "Married";
> For the LORD delights in you,
> And to Him your land will be married.
> For as a young man marries a virgin,
> So your sons will marry you;
> And as the bridegroom rejoices over the bride,
> So your God will rejoice over you.

---

[602] Revelation 4:8-11, 5:11-14
[603] Luke 24:53

Those who worship God are able to come close to Him through the atoning blood sacrifice of Jesus. Barricades and other ceremonial or legal barriers no longer separate us from God. We are now able to enter into the place where God Himself dwells, into His presence.[604] (Of course, since God is a spiritual being, we won't actually see THE LORD in front of us when we worship.) Jesus's sacrifice on the cross allows us direct access to God, and so, when we are in His presence, our worship ought to be suitable. Therefore, "let us show gratitude, by which we may offer to God an acceptable service with reverence and awe" (Hebrews 12:28). James 4:8 says, "Draw near to God and He will draw near to you. Cleanse your hands, you sinners; and purify your hearts, you double-minded." In drawing close to God, we may also "receive mercy and find grace to help in time of need" (Hebrews 4:16). In I Peter 2:5, the apostle says that those who worship in turn are "being built up as a spiritual house for a holy priesthood, to offer up spiritual sacrifices acceptable to God through Jesus Christ." As a result, even as we worship THE LORD, He does not stop giving to us.

Since worship is the primary activity of those already in Heaven, it is clear that it has great value and that that value is priceless and timeless. Worship of God brings you into His presence and God thus draws closer to you, giving you the benefits just mentioned. Hence, how we use our time on earth is very, very important because when we consume our time with non-worship activities, we are not fulfilling the purpose for which God created us. Particularly in the modern era, there are endless distractions that allow us to waste time. Pay attention to what Paul says in Ephesians 5:15-20:

> Therefore be careful how you walk, not as unwise men but as wise, *making the most of your time*, because the days are evil. So then *do not be foolish, but understand what the will of the Lord is*. And do not get drunk with wine, for that is dissipation, but be filled with the Spirit,

---

[604] Hebrews 10:19

speaking to one another in psalms and hymns and spiritual songs, singing and making melody with your heart to the Lord; *always giving thanks* for all things in the name of our Lord Jesus Christ to God, even the Father. (emphasis added)

What Paul is essentially saying is that you should not waste your time "getting drunk" with worldly things. Rather, set your mind on Godly things and on *continuously* giving praise and thanks to God.

People worship in a physical sense, but the primary realm of worship is the *spiritual* realm. John 4:23-24 says, "But an hour is coming, and now is, when the true worshipers will worship the Father in spirit and truth; for such people the Father seeks to be His worshipers. God is spirit, and those who worship Him must worship in spirit and truth." Worship in a general sense can involve many varieties of natural activities, but *true* worship is always a spiritual activity hidden to the human eye. For example, when Mary visited Elizabeth and was pregnant with Jesus, she praised God by saying, "My *soul* exalts the Lord, / And my *spirit* has rejoiced in God my Savior" (italics mine, Luke 1:46-47). So while Mary was praising God in a natural sense, she was also aware of a deeper act of worship in the spiritual realm. Consequently, worship *can* look like what most people would expect. Examples include people alone in their residences, lifting up their hands and praising God, or others in church, singing along with their fellow worshippers to a joyful song to THE LORD. However, since Jesus tells us that true worship is in "spirit and truth," our global thoughts and actions are also a form of worship. Moreover, if we ought to worship *in* the truth, we also know that the Word of God *is* the truth.[605] Therefore, learning and obeying the Word of God is also a form of worship. Furthermore, worshipping in the spirit nurtures the fruits of the spirit: love, joy, peace, patience, kindness, goodness, faithfulness, gentleness and self-control.[606]

---

[605] Proverbs 30:3; Psalm 33:4; John 17:17; II Timothy 2:15; Hebrews 4:12
[606] Galatians 5:22-23

Wayne Grudem says, "Genuine worship is not something that is self-generated or that can be worked up within ourselves. It must rather be the outpouring of our hearts *in response* to a realization of who God is."[607] As with everything else we have learned so far, it all begins with God. Otherwise, an atheist could begin "worshipping" God without any knowledge of who He really is. The seraphim in Isaiah 6:3 praise God due to their realization of Who He is: "Holy, Holy, Holy, is the LORD of hosts, / The whole earth is full of His glory." In other words, knowing Who God is and truly understanding all the marvelous things Jesus has done for us inspires a sense of awe and reverence for God in us. The result is genuine worship. One example is that of Matthew 14, where the disciples see Jesus walking on water and calming the winds. Verse 33 of the text says, "[T]hose who were in the boat worshiped Him, saying, 'You are certainly God's Son!'"

Because worship is a spiritual matter, it requires spiritual preparation (i.e. prayer), spiritual care and spiritual execution. A worship problem is, thus, a spiritual problem and requires spiritual answers. Also, before one can engage in genuine worship, he or she must reconcile any interpersonal problems[608] and family quarrels,[609] and diligently ensure that the church has not succumbed to "roots of bitterness."[610] Genuine worship is orderly[611] and is performed by those who have a pure heart[612] and strive for holiness.[613]

---

[607] Wayne Grudem, *Systematic Theology* (Grand Rapids: Zondervan, 1994), 1011.
[608] Matthew 5:24; I Timothy 2:8; I John 4:20
[609] I Peter 3:7
[610] Hebrews 12:15
[611] I Corinthians 14:33
[612] Matthew 5:8; I John 3:21; c.f. James 4:8
[613] Hebrews 12:14

www.ingramcontent.com/pod-product-compliance
Lightning Source LLC
LaVergne TN
LVHW041618070426
835507LV00008B/309